Felix Octavius Carr Darley, Nathan Boughton Warren

The Holidays

Christmas, Easter and Whitsuntide

Felix Octavius Carr Darley, Nathan Boughton Warren

The Holidays
Christmas, Easter and Whitsuntide

ISBN/EAN: 9783337380120

Printed in Europe, USA, Canada, Australia, Japan

Cover: Foto ©Lupo / pixelio.de

More available books at **www.hansebooks.com**

THE HOLIDAYS:

Christmas, Easter, and Whitsuntide;

THEIR

SOCIAL FESTIVITIES, CUSTOMS, AND CAROLS.

BY

NATHAN B. WARREN.

ILLUSTRATED BY F. O. C. DARLEY.

"I like them well, — the curious preciseness
And all pretended gravity of those
That seek to banish hence these harmless sports,
Have thrust away much ancient honesty."
London Holiday Book.

NEW YORK:
PUBLISHED BY HURD AND HOUGHTON.
Cambridge: Riverside Press.

Entered according to Act of Congress, in the year 1868, by
NATHAN B. WARREN,
in the Clerk's Office of the District Court for the Northern District of New York.

RIVERSIDE, CAMBRIDGE:
STEREOTYPED AND PRINTED BY
H. O. HOUGHTON AND COMPANY.

PREFACE.

SINCE the publication of Bourne's "Antiquitates Vulgares," or "Popular Antiquities," 1725, and its enlargement and republication by Brand and Sir Henry Ellis, many curious and entertaining works have appeared on this interesting subject. Among the most celebrated of these are the works of Hone, Strutt, Drake, Soane, Sandys, Wright, and Chambers. From these and others, also of high authority, but not quite so well known, the present volume on "The Holidays," has been compiled. If it shall help to meet what appears to be a literary want in this country, the writer will feel himself well rewarded for the labor bestowed upon the work. There appears to be a growing interest in the subject, owing, perhaps, to its connection with the great religious movement now progressing within the Church of England, whose influence is felt far beyond the strict limits of its communion. The social festivity which once always accompanied the observance of ecclesiastical festivals, whether under the Jewish or Christian dispensation, has at least the merit of interesting the young and of making an impression on the mind, which increasing years do not easily efface.

Zion's ways, like those of Wisdom, are indeed " ways of pleasantness, and all her paths are peace," to such at least as do not stray from them, and who can use without abusing the good gifts of a beneficent Creator.

It is hoped that the excellence of the illustrations of this work, both pictorial and choral, together with the quaint sayings of the old authors quoted, will make up for the deficiencies which may appear either in the plan or its execution.

N. B. W.

IDA COTTAGE, Troy, N. Y.,
November 5, 1868.

CONTENTS.

CHAP.		PAGE
I.	Introduction	1
II.	Origin of the Social Festivities of Christmas	7
III.	Christmas Carols	14
IV.	Christmas in the Halls of Old England	32
V.	Christmas Mummeries	45
VI.	Christmas Gambols	58
VII.	The Christmas Banquets of the Olden Time	69
VIII.	Twelfth-Day, or Old Christmas	80
IX.	Shrove-Tide or Carnival	90
X.	Easter	99
XI.	Rogation Week	110
XII.	Whitsuntide	122
XIII.	May Day	132
XIV.	St. John's or Midsummer Eve	146
XV.	Harvest Home	164

APPENDIX.

Gloria in Excelsis	174
The First Noel	176
Christmas Day in the Morning	179
As Joseph was a Walking	180
The Holy Well	181
The Holly and the Ivy	182
The Boar's Head Carol	186
Christmas Plays	188

INITIALS.

	PAGE
VILLAGERS AROUND THE MAY-POLE	1
BRINGING IN THE YULE-LOG	7
PIFFERARI	14
ROWENA PRESENTING THE WASSAIL BOWL TO VORTIGER	32
THE CHRISTMAS TREE	45
SNAP-DRAGON	58
COMBAT OF THE OXONIAN WITH THE WILD BOAR IN THE FOREST OF SHOTOVER	69
KING AND QUEEN OF THE BEAN	80
PANCAKE TOSSING IN WESTMINSTER SCHOOL	90
WOMEN HEAVING THE MEN AT EASTER	99
PARISH OFFICERS BEATING THE BOUNDS	110
ARCHERY EXHIBITION AT WHITSUNTIDE	122
RAISING OF THE MAY-POLE	132
ST. JOHN'S EVE	146
HARVEST HOME	164

ILLUSTRATIONS.

HARVEST HOME	*Frontispiece.*
CHRISTMAS WAIT	31
LORD OF MISRULE	64
CHRISTMAS BANQUET	71
WHITSUN ALE	130
A LONDON MARCHING WATCH ON MIDSUMMER'S EVE	153

CHAPTER I.

INTRODUCTION.

GREGORY the Great, in the oft-quoted letter to Mellitus, a British abbot (afterward a successor of Augustine in the See of Canterbury), says: "Whereas the people were accustomed to sacrifice many oxen in honor of demons, let them celebrate a religious and solemn festival, and not slay the animals, '*diabolo*'—'to the devil,' but to be eaten by themselves '*ad laudem Dei*,'—'to the Praise of God.'"

INTRODUCTION.

This idea seems to have been suggested to this Patron of the Anglo-Saxon Church by the success of a very similar experiment or transformation, which in an earlier age had resulted in the conversion to Christianity of the populous district of Neo-Cæsarea in Pontus. For it is said that Gregory, Bishop of that Diocese, changed the observance of the Pagan festivals to those of the Christian saints and martyrs, retaining such of their ancient festivities and ceremonies, as were in themselves harmless and to which the people were greatly attached. Objections to compliances such as these have been made by the precise and scrupulous both in ancient and modern times. Thus we read that Gregory Nazianzen and other Fathers of the Church, warned their flocks against the secularizing tendency of their age, and the dangers of excess in feasting, dancing, crowning the doors, and like practices. They feared that these things would carry their people back into Paganism or Judaism, not perceiving that Paganism had died a natural death, and that Judaism had been superseded by Christianity — the Law being indeed the shadow of good things to come. However this may be, Gregory the Great, undeterred by these serious apprehensions expressed by the early Fathers, and considering the wants of human nature, and especially those of his spiritual children, recommended, as we have seen, to the Anglo-Saxon missionaries, commissioned by him, a more liberal course in regard to these festivities, which appears to have greatly promoted the social well-being of the Anglo-Saxon race.

St. Augustine and the other Roman missionaries derived no inconsiderable assistance from the Calendar they found already in existence among their heathen converts. For the great Pagan festivals of the ancient world were regulated by the sun, their Feast of Yule, or "Juul," being about the winter solstice, or Christmas; the Festival of Eoster, or Easter, about the Vernal Equinox; and that of Midsummer, or St. John Baptist's Day, at the summer solstice. These most ancient of the world's festivals, under changed names and with new objects, are still kept in our own times. We are not, however, warranted in concluding from the above, as many archæologists have affirmed, that the social festivities of the Christian holidays are altogether of heathen origin, but, on the contrary, it will appear that they claim for themselves a much higher authority. In answer to certain Puritanical objections, of the kind just alluded to, we quote from a rare tract of 1648, entitled " The Vindication of the Solemnity of the Nativity of Christ " : —

" If it doth appeare that the time of this festival doth comply with the time of the Heathen's *Saturnalia*, this leaves no charge of impiety upon it, for since things are best cured by their contraries, it was both wisdom and piety in the ancient Christians (whose work it was to convert the Heathens from such, as well as other superstitions and miscarriages), to vindicate such times from the service of the Devil, by appoynting them to the more solemne and especiall service of God."

4   INTRODUCTION.

Moreover, it appears that our Christmas, Easter, and Whitsun festivals, have taken the place of those three great feasts of the Jewish Church, — the feasts of Passover, of Weeks, and of Tabernacles, instituted by Divine appointment. In the social festivities of the most joyous of these festivals, the Feast of Tabernacles, there is a striking resemblance to those of our Christmas holidays. The requirements of The Law, with respect to the Feast of Tabernacles, were: —

"And thou shalt rejoice in thy feast, thou, and thy son, and thy daughter, and thy manservant, and thy maidservant, and the Levite, the stranger, and the fatherless, and the widow, that are within thy gates. Seven days shalt thou keep a solemn feast unto the Lord thy God in the place which the Lord shall choose: because the Lord thy God shall bless thee in all thine increase, and in all the works of thine hands, therefore thou shalt surely rejoice." — *Deut.* xvi. 14, 15.

Smith, in his "Dictionary of the Bible," gives an interesting account of the manner in which this injunction of Moses was observed in after-times by the Jews in Jerusalem. He says: —

"Though all the Hebrew Annual Festivals were seasons of rejoicing, the Feast of Tabernacles was in this respect distinguished above them all. The huts and the *lûlâbs* must have made a gay and striking spectacle over the city by day; and the lamps, the flambeaux, the music, and the joyous gatherings in the court of the Temple, must have given a still more festive character to the night. . . . . At the Temple in the evening (after the day with which the festivals had commenced, had ended), both men and women assembled in the Court of the Women, expressly to hold a rejoicing for the drawing of the water of Siloam. On this occasion

INTRODUCTION. 5

a degree of unrestrained hilarity was permitted, such as would have been unbecoming while the ceremony itself was going on, in the presence of the Altar, and in connection with the offering of the Morning Sacrifice. . . . . . At the same time there were set up in the Court two lofty stands, each supporting four great lamps. These were lighted on each night of the Festival; and, as it is said, they cast their light over nearly the whole compass of the city. Many in the assembly carried flambeaux; a body of Levites stationed on the fifteen steps leading up to the Women's Court, played instruments of music and chanted the fifteen psalms (120 to 134), which are called in the A. V. 'Songs of Degrees.' Singing and dancing were afterwards continued for some time; the same ceremonies in the day, and the same joyous meetings in the evening, were renewed on each of the seven days."

The austerity and intolerance of the seventeenth century in regard to social festivities, have, in a great measure, given place in modern times to more rational ideas.

The learned, it appears, to the confusion of Judaizing zealots of the old Puritanical school, have clearly established the fact that the Jewish Festivals were, even in the time of our Saviour and his Apostles, seasons of general social enjoyment. In conformity with the positive injunctions of the Mosaic Law, the New Moons, the Passover, the Feast of Pentecost and of Tabernacles, were observed with a degree of hilarity altogether inconsistent with the modern Puritanical notions of propriety. Indeed, they applied very literally the words of the Psalmist, "Serve the Lord with gladness and come before his presence with a song."

It seems, therefore, reasonable to conclude that, as

INTRODUCTION.

Our Saviour went up regularly to these feasts at Jerusalem, and as the Apostles also continued even after his Ascension and the outpouring of the Spirit on the Day of Pentecost, to take part in these national festivals, there was nothing in these holiday festivities inconsistent with the profession of the principles of Christianity; for "they continuing daily with one accord in the Temple, and breaking bread from house to house, did eat their meat with gladness and singleness of heart."

The severity of our Puritanical forefathers in imagining the social festivities of their times to be merely heathenish vanities, is equaled only by their misconception in regard to the character of the Jewish holidays.[1] This mistake of theirs, however, is not more remarkable than that made by the Roman historian Tacitus, who erroneously supposed that the Jewish Feast of Tabernacles, held at the time of the vintage (in October), was celebrated in honor of Bacchus.

[1] The joyous nature of the Jewish festivals has been briefly but forcibly depicted by the author of *Festivals, Games, and Amusements*, in the following passage: "The sacred ceremonies which, exclusive of the pomp of sacrifice, the perfume of rich odors, and a stately display of gorgeously attired processionists in the courts of their venerated temple, and in the presence of a whole assembled people, combined the attractions of male and female dancers with all the enchantments of the most exquisite musicians and singers, were not only incomparably more grand, imposing, and magnificent, as a mere spectacle, than any theatrical exhibition that the world could produce, but appealed to the heart while they delighted the eye; gratified the soul as well as the sense; awakened feelings of patriotism as well as religion, and by uniting the splendors of earth to the glorious hopes of heaven, constituted a union of fascinations which no sensitive or pious Jew could have contemplated without an ecstasy of delight."

CHAPTER II.

ORIGIN OF THE SOCIAL FESTIVITIES OF CHRISTMAS.

BRADY, in his "Clavis Calendaria," says:—

"The first Christians, who, it is proper to remark, were all converts from the Hebrews, solemnized the Nativity on the first of January, conforming in this computation to the Roman year, though it is to be particularly noticed, that on the day of the Feast of Tabernacles they ornamented their churches with green boughs, as a memorial that Christ was actually born at that time, in like manner as the ancient Jews erected booths or tents which they inhabited at this season, to keep up by an express command from God the remembrance of their deliverance from Egyptian bondage, and of their having dwelt in tents or tabernacles in the wilderness."

The religious observance of Christmas[1] dates from a period as early, at least, as the Second Century. Haydn says it was first observed A. D. 98. Clement, the co-worker of St. Paul, mentioned by him in his Epistle to the Philippians (iii. 3), says: " Brethren, keep diligently feast days ; and truly in the first place the day of Christ's birth."

It was ordered to be kept as a solemn Feast, and with the performance of Divine Services, on the 25th of December, by Telesphorus, Bishop of Rome, about A. D. 137. His injunctions are, "that in the holy night of the Nativity of our Lord and Saviour, they do celebrate public Church services, and in them solemnly sing the Angels' Hymn, because also the same night he was declared unto the shepherds by an angel, as the truth itself doth witnesse." In the same age Theophilus, Bishop of Cæsarea, recommends " the celebration of the birth-day of Our Lord, on what day soever the 25th of December shall happen." In the following century, Cyprian begins his "Treatise on the Nativity," thus: " The much wished for and long expected Nativity of Christ is come, the famous solemnity is come."

Gregory Nazianzen and St. Basil both have sermons

---

[1] The term "Christmas" is derived from *Christ* and the Saxon *maisse*, signifying the Mass, and a Feast.

on this day. St. Chrysostom also says: "This day was of great antiquity, and of long continuance, being famous and renowned in the Church from the beginning, far and wide, from Thrace as far as Gades in Spain." And he styles it, "the most venerable and tremendous of all festivals, and the Metropolis or Mother of all Festivals."

Blunt, also, in his "Annotated Book of Common Prayer," observes: —

"Most of the Fathers have left sermons which were preached on Christmas Day, or during the continuance of the festival. And secular decrees of the Christian emperors, as well as canons of the Church, show, that it was very strictly observed as a time of rest from labour, of Divine Worship, and of Christian hilarity, and that 'it is most fit that the season so marked out by angels by songs of joy such as had not been heard on Earth since the Creation, should also be observed as a time of festive gladness by the Church, and in the social life of Christians."

This hilarity and festive gladness — the marked peculiarity of an old English Christmas — once included sundry pageants and religious shows, which, in an age less cultivated than our own, combined for the people instruction and amusement, the clergy in them, as it were, teaching the multitude by a sort of parables.

After the invention of printing, however, when better means of popular instruction became possible, these mysteries and moralities gradually degenerated into mere burlesques, masks, or mummeries, which frequently, it appears, proved to be more or less objectionable, and against which the Puritanism of the Sixteenth and Seventeenth Centuries maintained an unceasing and destructive warfare; nevertheless there still survives in these prosaic days, especially in those hospitable mansions wherein "Christmas yearly dwells," and where —

> "Numerous guests and viands dainty,
> Fill the hall, and grace the board,"

much of that hilarity which, indeed, is the essential part of the festival.

The bringing in and placing of the ponderous Christmas-block, or Yule-log, on the hearth of the wide chimney of the Old English Hall, was the most joyous of the ceremonies observed on Christmas Eve. This mode of rejoicing at the Winter Solstice, appears to have originated with the Danes and Pagan Saxons, and was intended to be emblematical of the return of the Sun, and its increasing light and heat. But on the introduction of Christianity, the illuminations of the *Eve of Yule* were continued as representative of the *True Light*, which was then ushered into the world, in the person of Our Saviour, the "DAY-SPRING FROM ON HIGH."

"This venerable Yule-log, destined to crackle a welcome to all comers, was drawn," says Mr. Chambers, "in triumph from its resting place at the feet of its living brethren of the woods. Each wayfarer raised his hat as it passed, for he well knew it was full of good promises, and that its flame would burn out old wrongs and heart-burnings."[1]

[1] In Devonshire this Yule-log takes the form of the Ashton fagot; the

The towns of England have been described by Stowe and other old writers as presenting at this season a sylvan appearance; the houses dressed with branches of ivy and holly; the churches converted into leafy tabernacles, and standards bedecked with evergreens set up in the streets, while the young of both sexes danced around them.

It is interesting to observe from such descriptions, the close resemblance between these manners and customs, and those described in the passages quoted from Smith and Brady; when, in accordance with Scripture injunctions, the people of Israel went forth into the mount and brought thence "olive-branches, and pine-branches, and myrtle-branches, and palm-branches, and branches of thick trees, and made themselves booths, every one upon the roof of his house, and in their courts, and in the courts of the house of God, and in the street of the water-gate, and in the street of the gate of Ephraim."

"The ancient custom of dressing our churches and houses at Christmas with evergreens, appears to be not only thus traceable to the Feast of Tabernacles, but is also supposed to have been derived from certain expressions in the following prophecies of the coming of our Saviour: 'Behold the days come, saith the Lord, that I will raise unto David a Righteous Branch;' 'For behold I will bring

---

Scandinavian tradition that man was created out of an ash-tree, may have originated the custom. The fagot is composed of a bundle of ash-sticks, bound or hooped round with bands of the same tree, and the number of these last ought, it is said, to be nine. It is an acknowledged and time-honored custom that for every *crack* which the bands of the ashen fagot made in bursting when charred through, the master of the house is bound to furnish a fresh bowl cf wassail.

forth my servant the Branch;' 'Thus speaketh the Lord of Hosts, saying, behold the Man whose name is The Branch, and He shall grow up out of his place; 'At that time will I cause the Branch of Righteousness to grow up unto David;' 'Thus saith the Lord God, I will also take of the highest Branch of the High Cedar, and will set it; I will crop off from the top of his young twigs a tender one, and will plant it upon an high mountain and eminent; in the mountain of the height of Israel will I plant it, and it shall bring forth boughs, and bear fruit, and it shall be a goodly Cedar;' 'In that day shall the Branch of the Lord be beautiful and glorious;' 'For He shall grow up before Him as a tender plant, and as a root out of a dry ground; and the Lord shall reign over them in Mount Zion from henceforth even for ever;' 'There shall come forth a rod out of the stem of Jesse, and a branch shall grow out of his roots, which shall stand for an ensign of the people, and my servant David shall be their Prince for ever.'

"For it must be confessed that those passages and expressions in which our Saviour is represented under the type of a Branch, a Righteous Branch, a Bough, the Branch of Righteousness, who will reign for ever, etc., in the above quoted clear and eminent prophecies of his first appearance in the flesh upon earth, are in a most lively manner brought to our memories, and unmistakably alluded to by those *branches* and *boughs* of evergreens, with which our churches and houses are adorned, whose gay appearance and perpetual verdure, in that dead season of the year, when all Nature looks comfortless, dark, and dreary, and when the rest of the vegetable world has shed its honors, does agreeably charm the unwearied beholder and make a very suitable accompaniment of the universal joy which always attends the annual commemoration of that holy festival." — See *Gentleman's Magazine*, 1765.

Another quaint old writer thus spiritualizes the practice of Christmas decoration: —

"So our churches and houses, decked with bayes and rosemary, holly and ivy, and other plants which are always green, winter and summer, signify and put us in mind of His Deity; that the Child who now was born was God and Man, who should spring up like a tender plant, should always be green and flourishing, and live for evermore."

In this custom there appears to be also a reference to those passages of the prophet Isaiah, which foretell the felicities attending the coming of Christ, namely: "The glory of Lebanon shall come unto thee, the fir-tree, the pine-tree, and the box, together, to *beautify the place of my sanctuary.*" (Isaiah lx. 13.) "Instead of the thorn, shall come up the fir-tree, and instead of the brier shall come up the myrtle-tree, and it shall be to the Lord for a name, for an everlasting sign that shall not be cut off."

In an old English custom described by Thomas Millar, we find a happy response to this prophecy of Isaiah:—

"The hundreds of silver-toned bells of London ring loud, deep, and clear, from tower and spire, to welcome in Christmas. The far-stretching suburbs, like glad children, take up and fling back the sound over hill and valley, marsh and meadow, while steeple calls to steeple across the winding arms of the mast-crowded river, proclaiming to the heathen voyager who has brought his treasures to our coast, and who is ignorant of our religion, the approach of some great Christian festival."

CHAPTER III.

CHRISTMAS CAROLS.

CAROL singing appears to have originated in a usage of the Primitive Church, for "In the early ages the bishops were accustomed to sing Carols on Christmas Day with their clergy." Jeremy Taylor, referring to this custom in his "Great Exemplar," says of the "*Gloria in Excelsis*,"[1] "As soon as those blessed choristers had sung their *Christmas Carol*, and taught the church a hymn to put into

[1] See Appendix.

her offices for ever in the anniversary of this Festivity, the angels returned into heaven."

The term "carol" is supposed to be derived either from the Italian "caroli" — a song of devotion, or carol, properly "a round dance."[1] Carols, it is said, were early introduced by the clergy into England from Italy, probably soon after the Norman Conquest, as a substitute for the Yule and Wassail songs of heathen origin, which, until then, had been in use among the vulgar. The custom of singing these "caroli" is still maintained in Italy; indeed, on the continent, caroling at Christmas is almost universal, and particularly in Rome, where, during the season of Advent, the Pifferari may be seen and heard performing their Novena before the shrine of the Madonna and Bambino. These pilgrims, who, by the way, are

---

[1] French *carole, querole;* Breton *keroll,* a dance ; Welsh *coroli,* to reel, to dance.

"Tho mightest thou karollis sene
And folke dance and merie ben,
And made many a faire tourning
Upon the green grass springing."
Romaunt of the Rose, A. D. 760.

Chanson de carole, a song accompanying a dance ; then, as French *balade,* from Italian *ballare,* to dance, applied to the song itself. Diez suggests *chorulus,* from *chorus,* as the origin. But we have no occasion to invent a diminutive, as the Latin *corolla,* from *corona,* gives the exact sense required. Robert of Brune calls the circuit of Druidical stones a carol."

"The Bretons ranged about the felde
The *karole* of the stones behelde,
Many tyme yede tham about,
Biheld within, biheld without."
Wedgewood's Dictionary.

shepherds from the Calabrian Mountains, annually flock to Rome at this season. Their picturesque costume is thus described in " Roba di Roma:"—

"On their heads they wear conical felt hats adorned with a frayed peacock's feather, or a faded band of red cords and tassels; their bodies are clad in red waistcoats, blue jackets, and small-clothes of skin or yellowish homespun cloth; skin sandals are bound to their feet with cords that interlace each other up the leg as far as the knee, — and over all is worn a long brown or blue cloak with a short cape, buckled closely round the neck. Sometimes, but rarely, this cloak is of a deep red with a scalloped cape. As they stand before the pictures of the Madonna, their hats placed on the ground before them, and their thick disheveled hair covering their sunburnt brows, blowing away on their instruments or pausing to sing their *novena*, they form a picture which every artist desires to paint. These Pifferari always go in couples, one playing on the zampogna or bagpipe, the base and treble accompaniment, and the other on the piffero, or pastoral pipe, which carries the air. Sometimes one of them varies the performance by singing, in a strong peasant voice, verse after verse of the *novena* to the accompaniment of the bagpipe."

But to return from this digression. The old English Yule songs before referred to, are mentioned by Brady in his " Calendaria " (1808). He says that in his time they were still sung by the people about the church-yards after service on Christmas Day. The example given by him is identical with that in the Christmas of Washington Irving's " Sketch Book."

"Ule, Ule, Ule, Ule,
 Three puddings in a pule,
 Crack nuts and cry Ule."

These Yule songs, it appears, were sung at the bringing in of the Christmas block, or Yule-log, which was anciently introduced into the old English baronial hall with much pomp and circumstance, the minstrels saluting its appearance with a song. The following specimen from the Sloane MS. is supposed to be of the time of Henry VI., and appears to have been a sort of intermediate link between the ancient Yule song and its more orthodox substitute, the Christmas Carol.

WELCOME YULE!

"Welcome be thou heavenly King,
Welcome, born on this morning,
Welcome for whom we shall sing,
Welcome Yule!

"Welcome be ye Stephen and John,
Welcome Innocents every one,
Welcome Thomas, Martyr-one,
Welcome Yule!

"Welcome be ye, good New Year,
Welcome Twelfth-Day, both in fere,
Welcome Saints, loved and dear,
Welcome Yule!

"Welcome be ye, Candlemas,
Welcome be ye Queen of Bliss,
Welcome both to more and less,
Welcome Yule!

> "Welcome be ye that are here,
> Welcome all, and make good cheer,
> Welcome all another year,
> Welcome Yule!"

The Carol for St. Stephen's Day, which follows this, founded on an ancient legend, is of the beginning of the fourteenth century. Very nearly the original words are given as a specimen of the language of the period. In the carol entitled "The Carnal and the Crane," this same legend appears in a more modern dress.

CAROL FOR ST. STEPHEN'S DAY.

> "Saint Stephen was a clerk
> In King Herode's hall,
> And served him of bread and cloth
> As ever king befalle.[1]

> "Stephen out of kitchen came
> With boar's head in hande,
> He saw a star was fair and bright,
> Over Bethlem stande.

> "He cast adown the boar's head,
> And went into the halle:—
> 'I forsake thee, King Herod,
> And thy werkes alle.

> "'I forsake thee, King Heroa,
> And thine werkes alle,
> There is a child in Bethlem borne,
> Is better than we alle.'

[1] Befalle, *i. e.*, happened;—as well as ever happened to a king.

"'What aileth thee, Stephen,
 What is thee befalle?
Lacketh thee either meat or drink,
 In King Herod's hall?'

"'Lacketh me neither meat nor drink
 In King Herod's hall,
There is a child in Bethlem borne,
 Is better than we all.'

"'What aileth thee, Stephen,
 Art thou wode,[1] or thou ginnest to brede?[2]
Lacketh thee either gold or fee,
 Or any rich weede?'[3]

"'Lacketh me neither gold nor fee,
 Nor none rich weede,
There is a child in Bethlem borne
 Shall help us at our need.'

"'That is all so sooth, Stephen,
 All so sooth, I wiss,
As this capon crow shall,
 That lyeth here in my dish.'

"That word was not so soon said,
 That word in that hall,
The capon crew, 'Christus natus est,'
 Among the lordes alle.

---

[1] Wode, *i. e.*, mad.
[2] Brede, *i. e.*, upbraid. Danish, "bebreide." In Chaucer the line,—"For veray wo out of his wit he braide," is explained, "He went, or ran out of his wits."
[3] Weede, *i. e.*, dress.

"Riseth up my tormentors,
 By two, and all by one,
And leadeth Stephen out of town,
 And stoneth him with stone.

"Token they Stephen,
 And stoned him in the way,
And therefore is his even,
 On Christe's owen day."

The custom of carol singing formerly prevailed over the greater part of the British Isles, and there are still in use in many places, especially among the peasantry of Derbyshire and Lancashire, Yorkshire, Northumberland, and Durham, carols of undoubted antiquity, illustrative of the manners and sentiments of the Middle Ages, some of which are said to be fragments of the Mystery and Miracle Plays, formerly enacted at this season. The following are selected as specimens from these curious old carols:—

AS JOSEPH WAS A-WALKING.[1]

"As Joseph was a-walking,
 He heard an angel sing,
'This night shall be the birth-time
 Of Christ the Heav'nly King.

"'He neither shall be born
 In housen nor in hall,
Nor in the place of Paradise,
 But in an ox's stall.

[1] For music see Appendix.

"'He neither shall be clothed
  In purple nor in pall,
But in the fair white linen
  That usen babies all.

"'He neither shall be rocked
  In silver nor in gold,
But in a wooden manger
  That resteth on the mould.'

"As Joseph was a-walking,
  There did an angel sing;
And Mary's child at midnight
  Was born to be our king.

"Then be ye glad good people,
  This night of all the year,
And light ye up your candles,
  For His star it shineth clear."

The next specimen seems to have been founded on a legend from one of the Apocryphal Gospels. It exhibits, says Mr. Howitt, a striking impress of the character of the Middle Ages, and shows how well they understood the true spirit of Christ. The music is to be found in the Appendix: —

THE HOLY WELL.

"Honor the leaves, and the leaves of life
  Upon this blest holiday,
When Jesus asked his mother dear
  Whether He might go to play.

"'To play! to play!' said Blessed Mary,
    'To play, then, get you gone;
And see there be no complaint of you
    At night when you come home.'

"Sweet Jesus He ran into yonder town
    As far as the Holy Well;
And there He saw three as fine children
    As ever eyes beheld.

"He said, 'God bless you every one,
    And sweet may your sleep be;
And now, little children, I'll play with you,
    And you shall play with Me.'

"'Nay, nay, we are Lords' and Ladies' sons—
    Thou art meaner than us all;
Thou art but a silly fair maid's child
    Born in an oxen's stall."

"Sweet Jesus turned Him around,
    And He neither laugh'd nor smiled,
But the tears came trickling from his eyes,
    Like water from the skies.

"Sweet Jesus He ran to his mother dear,
    As fast as He could run—
'O mother, I saw three as fine children
    As ever were eyes set on.

"'I said, "God bless you every one,
    And sweet may your sleep be;
And now, little children, I'll play with you,
    And you shall play with Me.'

"' "Nay," said they, "we're Lords' and Ladies' sons,
　　Thou art meaner than us all;
　For thou art but a poor fair maid's child,
　　Born in an oxen's stall."'

"' Though you are but a maiden's child
　　Born in an oxen's stall,
　Thou art the Christ, the King of Heaven,
　　And the Saviour of them all.

"' Sweet Jesus, go down to yonder town,
　　As far as the Holy Well,
　And take away those sinful souls
　　And dip them deep in hell.'

"' Nay, nay,' ' sweet Jesus said,
　　' Nay, nay, that may not be,
　For there are too many sinful souls
　　Crying out for the help of Me.'[1]

"O, then spoke the Angel Gabriel,
　　Upon one good Saint Stephen,
　' Although you're but a maiden's child,
　　You are the King of Heaven.'

Numeral Hymns were common in the olden time. The following is one of the most ancient of all the popular carols; the original, preserved among the Sloane MSS., and of a date not later than the fourteenth century, is entitled —

---

[1] This response seems to have been suggested by the answer made by Christ to the disciples when they would have called down fire from heaven. — *Luke* ix. 54, 55.

"JOYES FYVE."

"The first good joy our Mary had,
　It was the joy of one,
To see her own Son Jesus
　To suck at her breast bone,
　To suck at her breast bone.
　　Good man, and blessed, may he be
　　　Both Father, Son, and Holy Ghost,
　　And Christ to eternity.

"The next good joy our Mary had,
　It was the joy of two,
To see her own Son Jesus
　To make the lame to go;
　To make the lame to go.
　　Good man, etc.

"The next good joy our Mary had,
　It was the joy of three,
To see her own Son Jesus
　To make the blind to see;
　To make the blind to see.
　　Good man, etc.

"The next good joy our Mary had,
　It was the joy of four,
To see her own Son Jesus
　To read the Bible o'er;
　To read the Bible o'er.
　　Good man, etc.

"The next good joy our Mary had,
　It was the joy of five,

To see her own Son Jesus
To raise the dead alive;
To raise the dead alive.
Good man, etc.

"The next good joy our Mary had,
It was the joy of six,
To see her own Son Jesus
To wear the crucifix;
To wear the crucifix.
Good man, etc.

"The next good joy our Mary had,
It was the joy of seven,
To see her own Son Jesus
To wear the crown of Heaven,
To wear the crown of Heaven.
Good man, and blessed may he be,
Both Father, Son, and Holy Ghost,
And Christ to eternity."

The following popular carol is from a Kentish version:—

CHRISTMAS DAY IN THE MORNING.

"I saw three ships come sailing in,
On Christmas Day, on Christmas Day;
I saw three ships come sailing in,
On Christmas Day in the morning.[1]

"And what was in those ships all three? etc.;
And what was in those ships all three? etc.

[1] In *singing* this carol, repeat after the first line of *each* verse, "On Christmas Day, on Christmas Day," and after the second line, "On Christmas Day in the morning."

"Our Saviour Christ and his ladie, etc.;
Our Saviour Christ and his ladie, etc.

"Pray whither sailed those ships all three? etc.;
Pray whither sailed those ships all three? etc.

"O they sailed into Bethlehem, etc.;
O they sailed into Bethlehem, etc.

"And all the bells on earth shall ring, etc.;
And all the bells on earth shall ring, etc.

"And all the Angels in Heaven shall sing, etc.;
And all the Angels in Heaven shall sing, etc.

"And all the Souls on Earth shall sing, etc.;
And all the Souls on Earth shall sing, etc.

"Then let us all rejoice amain, etc.;
Then let us all rejoice amain, etc."

Ritson thinks that the different versions of this carol may have had their origin in the following curious fragment found by him in Scotland:—

"There comes a ship far sailing then,
Saint Michel was the stieres-man;
Saint John sate in the horn:
Our Lord harped, our Lady sang,
And all the bells of heaven they rang,
On Christ's Sonday at morn."

The carol entitled "The Holly and the Ivy," is from Sylvester's collection, and is derived from an old broadside printed more than a century and a half ago. The holly, from time immemorial, has been the favorite Christmas evergreen. Dr. Turner, an early English writer on plants, calls it "holy" and "holy-tree;" which appellation was given it, most probably, from its being used in holy places. "It has a great variety of names in Germany, amongst which is *Christdorn;* in Danish it is also called *Christhorn;* and in Swedish *Christtorn*, amongst other appellations; from whence it appears that it is considered a holy plant, by many people in those countries."

THE HOLLY AND THE IVY.[1]

"The Holly and the Ivy
Now are both well grown,
Of all the trees that are in the wood,
The holly bears the crown.
Chorus. — The rising of the sun,
The running of the deer,
The playing of the merry organ,
The singing in the choir.

"The holly bears a blossom
As white as the lily flower,
And Mary bore sweet Jesus Christ,
To be our sweet Saviour.
Chorus. — The rising of the sun, etc.

"The holly bears a berry,
As red as any blood,

[1] Music in the Appendix.

And Mary bore sweet Jesus Christ,
    To do poor sinners good.
Chorus. — The rising of the sun, etc.

"The holly bears a prickle
    As sharp as any thorn,
And Mary bore sweet Jesus Christ,
    On Christmas Day in the morn.
Chorus. — The rising of the sun, etc.

"The holly bears a bark,
    As bitter as any gall,
And Mary bore sweet Jesus Christ,
    For to redeem us all.
Chorus. — The rising of the sun, etc.

"The holly and the ivy
    Now are both well grown,
Of all the trees that are in the wood,
    The holly bears the crown.
Chorus. — The rising of the sun," etc.

So popular had carols such as these become in the fifteenth century, that Wynkyn de Worde, one of the earliest printers, published a collection of them in 1521, containing among others, the celebrated "Boar's Head Carol," the best in the collection;[1] for besides the devotional carols in use at the season, there were those of a convivial character. These "jolie carols," as old Tusser calls them, were sung by the company or by itinerant minstrels who attended the feasts for the purpose.

[1] See Appendix for the music of this famous carol.

The Reformation, it appears, did not by any means impair the popularity of the Christmas Carol in England. Says an old writer of 1631, "Suppose Christmas now approaching, the evergreen ivy trimming and adorning the portals and partcloses of so frequented a building; the *usual carols* to observe antiquity cheerfully sounding, and that which is the complement of his inferior comforts, his neighbors, whom he tenders as members of his own family, join with him in this consort of mirth and melody."

One of these Christmas Carols, printed about the same period, recites some of the peculiar *pastimes* of the season : —

> "Hark how the wagges abroad doe call
> Each other forthe to rambling;
> Anon you'll see them in the hall
> For nuts and apples scrambling;
> The wenches, with their wassail bowles
> About the streets are singing;
> The boyes are come to catch the owles,
> The wild mare is in bringing."

Mr. Davies Gilbert has, in a collection of ancient Christmas Carols, said, that "Till recently in the West of England on Christmas Eve, about seven or eight o'clock in the evening, cakes were drawn hot from the oven; cider or beer exhilarated the spirits in every house; and the singing of carols was continued late in the night. On Christmas Day these carols took the place of psalms in all the churches, especially at afternoon service, the whole congregation joining; and at the end it was usual for the parish clerk to declare, in a loud voice, his wishes for a merry Christmas and a happy New Year, to all the parishioners."

In Wales Christmas caroling is still kept up, perhaps to a greater extent even than in England. After the turn of midnight on Christmas Eve, divine service is celebrated, followed by the singing of carols to the harp; and they are also with similar accompaniment sung in the *houses*, during the continuance of the Christmas holidays.

The instruments used by the waits at Christmas in old times, consisted ordinarily of hautboys of four different sizes, although Morley's "Consort Lessons," dedicated to the Lord Mayor and Aldermen of London, 1529, speak of the treble and base viols, the flute, the cittern or English guitar, the treble lute, and the pandora.

This ancient custom of carol singing at Christmas, is one of those which of late years has greatly revived and become generally popular both in Europe and America. The usage, however, in regard to their performance, has been made to conform in great measure to our modern notions of propriety and convenience. Itinerant minstrels, during the season of Advent, do not now often awaken people from their slumbers at midnight with a carol similar to that of —

"God rest you merry gentlemen,
Let nothing you dismay!"

Nor do the "waits" (those famous bands of vocal and instrumental performers) go now as they once did, from house to house, and from hamlet to hamlet, "all the night long, chanting such carols as our pious forefathers loved well to listen to." Nocturnes such as these with pastoral symphonies, performed by such shepherd-like swains, are altogether too romantic for these more prosaic days. And yet Keble, that most popular of modern poets, has piously sung : —

"Wake me that I the twelvemonth long,
   May bear the song
About me in the world's throng ;
That treasured joys of Christmas tide
May with mine hour of gloom abide ;
   The Christmas Carol ring
Deep in my heart, when I would sing,
Each of the twelve good days,
Its earnest yield of duteous love and praise,
Ensuring happy months, and hallowing common ways."

NOTE. — In France, "Noel" is the term used to express Christmas songs or carols, as well as the tide of Yule itself. This word *noel* is commonly understood to be derived from the Latin *natalis* (the *dies natalis* of Our Lord), and is said by Mr. Wright to have been introduced into England at the time of the Norman Conquest.

CHAPTER IV.

CHRISTMAS IN THE HALLS OF OLD ENGLAND.

Christmas Carols, as is observed in the preceding chapters, were divided into two classes; the more serious of them, those of a religious character, were sung morning and evening; and those which were convivial in their nature, at those bountiful and stately banquets in which our English ancestors so greatly delighted, and which were indeed the especial glory of the Christmas holidays.[1]

[1] For examples, see Appendix.

Some account of those Gothic halls in which these Christmas festivities were held, might, it is supposed, add to the interest of the present work. The following facts are derived chiefly from Mr. Thomas Wright's learned work, entitled " Domestic Manners and Sentiments of the Middle Ages."

First we learn that the most important part of the Saxon house was the hall. It was the place where the household collected round their lord and protector; and where the visits of a stranger were first received — the scene of hospitality. These Saxon dwellings appear to have been of wood, of which material houses continued very generally to be built, until comparatively modern times. A great change, however, was wrought in England by the entrance of the Normans. Some time after that period, or about the middle of the twelfth century, we begin to become better acquainted with the domestic manners of our forefathers, and from this time to the end of the fourteenth century the change was very gradual, and in many respects the manners and customs remained nearly the same. The "hall," or, according to the Norman word, the "salle," was still the principal part of the building; but its old Saxon character seems to have been so universally acknowledged that the first or Saxon name prevailed over the other. The name at this time usually given to the whole dwelling-house, was the Norman word "manoir," or manor; and we find this applied popularly to the houses of all classes, excepting only the cottages of laboring people.

In houses of the twelfth century, the hall, situated on the ground floor, and open to the roof, continued to form the principal feature of the building. A chamber generally adjoined one end, and at the other was usually a stable. The whole building stood within a small inclosure, consisting, in front, of a yard or court, called in Norman "aire" (area); and in the rear, of a garden which was surrounded with a hedge and ditch. In front, the house had generally one door, which was the main entrance into the hall, from which apartment there was a door into the chamber at one end; and one into the "croiche," or stable, at the other end, and a back door into the garden. The stable, as a matter of course, would have a large door, or outlet into the yard. The chief windows were those of the hall.

Alexander Neckam, Abbot of Cirencester, who died in 1217, has left us a sufficiently clear description of the Norman hall. He says that it had a vestibule or screen (vestibulum), and was entered through a porch (porticus), and that it had a court (atrium). In the interior of the hall, there were posts (or columns) placed at regular distances. The few examples of Norman halls which remain, are thus divided internally by two rows of these columns. He enumerates the materials required in the construction of the hall, which shows that he is speaking of a timber building. A fine example of one of these timber halls, though of a later period, is, or was recently, standing in the city of Gloucester, with its internal posts as here described. There appears, also, to have been an inner court-yard, in which Neckam intimates that poultry were kept. The whole building and the two court-yards were surrounded by a wall, outside of which were the garden and orchard.

At the close of the fourteenth century, the middle classes of England had made great advances in wealth and independence. This increase of wealth appears in the multiplication of articles of furniture and household implements, especially those of a more valuable description. There was also a great increase both in the number and magnitude of the houses which intervened between the castle and the cottage. Instead of having one or two bedrooms only, and turning people at night into the hall to sleep, as in earlier times, we now find whole suites of chambers; while, where before, the family lived chiefly in the hall, privacy was now sought by the addition of parlors, of which there were often more than one, in a house of ordinary size. The hall was, in fact, already beginning to diminish in relative importance to the rest of the mansion. Whether in town or country, houses of any magnitude were now generally built round an interior court, into which the rooms almost invariably looked, only small and unimportant windows looking toward the street or country. This arrangement, of course, originated in the necessity of studying security, a necessity which was never felt in England more severely than during the fifteenth century.

The hall was still but scantily furnished. The permanent furniture consisted chiefly of benches and of a seat with a back to it, for the superior members of the family. The head table, at least, which stood on a dais, or raised platform, at the upper end of the hall, was often a permanent one; and there were in general other permanent tables, or "tables dormants;" but still the majority of the tables in the hall were made up for each meal, by placing boards upon trestles. Cushions with ornamental cloths called " bankers " and " dorsers," for placing over the benches and backs of the seats of the better persons at the table, were also in general use. On special occasions tapestry was suspended on the walls of the hall. Another article of furniture also had now become common, the "buffet," or stand on which the plate and other vessels were arranged.

A vocabulary of the fifteenth century enumerates as the ordinary furniture of the hall: "A board, a trestle, a banker, a dorser, a natte (table-cloth), a table dormant, a basin, a laver, fire on a hearth, a brand or torch, a Yule block, an andiron, tongs, a pair of bellows, wood for the fire, a long settle, a chair, a bench, a stool, a cushion, and a screen."

There were also "waits," or trumpeters, in olden time always attached to the halls of great people, to announce the commencement of the dinner. Only persons of a certain rank were allowed this piece of ostentation; but everybody who could obtain it had minstrelsy at dinner. The wandering minstrel was welcome in every hall; and for this very reason the class of ambulatory musicians was very numerous.

In the sixteenth century the hall still continued to hold its position as the great public apartment of the house, and in its arrangements it differed slightly from those of an earlier date; it was, indeed, now, the only part of the house which had not been affected by the increasing taste for domestic privacy. We have many examples of the old Gothic hall of this period in England, not only as it existed and was used in the sixteenth century, but in some cases, especially in colleges, still used for its original purposes. One of the simplest, and at the same time best examples of these halls, is found in the Hospital of St. Cross near Winchester : —

"The principal entrance to the main building from the first or outer court, opened into a *thorough lobby*, having on one side several doors or arches leading to the buttery, kitchen, and domestic offices ; on the other side, the hall, parted off by a screen, generally of wood elaborately carved, and enriched with shields and a variety of ornament, and pierced with several arches having folding doors. Above the screen and over the lobby, was the minstrels' gallery, and on its front were usually hung armor, antlers, and similar memorials of the family exploits. The hall itself was a large and lofty room, in the shape of a parallelogram ; the roof, the timbers of which were framed with pendents, richly carved and emblazoned with heraldic insignia, formed one of its most striking features. 'The top-beam of the hall' — in allusion to the position of his coat of arms — was a symbolical manner of drinking the health of the master of the house. At the upper end of this chamber — furthest from the entrance — the floor was usually raised a step, and this part was styled the 'dais', or 'high place.' On one side of the dais was a deep embayed window, reaching nearly down to the floor; the other windows ranged along one or both sides of the hall, at a considerable height above the ground, so as to leave room for wainscoting or arras below them. They were enriched with stained glass, representing the armorial bearings of the family, their connections, and royal patrons, and between the windows were hung full length portraits of the same persons. The royal arms, also, usually occupied a conspicuous station at either end of the room. The head table was laid for the lord and principal guests on the raised place, parallel with the upper end wall, and other tables were ranged along the sides for inferior visitors and retainers. Tables so placed were said to stand 'banquet-wise.' In the centre of the hall was the rere-dosse, or fire-iron, against which fagots were piled, and burnt upon the stone floor; the smoke passing through an aperture in the roof immediately overhead, which was generally formed into an elevated lantern, a conspicuous ornament to the exterior of the building. In latter times a wide arched fire-place was formed in the wall on one side of the room."

The earlier half of the sixteenth century was the period when the pageantry of feasting in these halls was carried to its greatest degree of splendor, especially at Christmas. "In the houses of the noble and wealthy, the dinner itself was laid out with great pomp, was almost always accompanied with music, and not unfrequently interrupted with dances, mummings, and masquerades."

In view of the above it is easy to form an idea of those domestic establishments in which our forefathers used to keep their Christmas. We say *our* forefathers, for although the old manorial residences belonged to the nobility and gentry of the land, yet the whole population may in a manner be said to have kept their Christmas there.

Everywhere, indeed, during the twelve days of Christmas, these old halls were the centres of holiday festivities. From time to time it appears that the gentry and nobility of the realm were admonished by royal authority of their duty to go down to their country seats, and then and there to entertain their friends and neighbors with liberal hospitality. Aubrey says of these times: —

"In the days of yore, lords and gentlemen lived in the country like petty kings; had jura regalia belonging to their seignories; had their castles and boroughs; had gallows within their liberties; where they could try, condemn, and execute; never went to London but in Parliament time, or once a year to do homage to the king. They always ate in Gothic halls at the high table or *orielle* (which is a little room at the upper end of the hall, where stands a table), with the folks at the side tables. The meat was served up by watchwords. Jacks are but a late invention."

Here in the hall the mumming, and the loaf-stealing, and other Christmas sports, were performed. The hearth was commonly in the middle, whence the saying —

"*Round about* our sea-coal fire."

Heretofore noblemen and gentlemen of fair estates had their heralds, who wore their coat-of-arms at Christmas, and at other solemn times, and cried " Largesse" thrice. The halls in fact, of all the colleges, at the Universities of Oxford and Cambridge, and in the Inns of Court, still remain, as in Aubrey's time, accurate examples of the ancient baronial and conventual halls; preserving not merely their original form and appearance, but the identical arrangement and service of the tables.

It is said that at Houghton Chapel, Nottinghamshire, "*the good Sir William Hollis*," that example of the "fine old English gentleman, all of the olden time,' who kept his house in great splendor and hospitality, began Christmas at All Hallow-tide (October 31), and continued it till Candlemas (February 2); during which time *any man* was permitted to stay three days, without being asked who he was, or whence he came.

In the "Diary" of the Rev. John Ward, Vicar of Stratford-upon-Avon, extending from 1648 to 1679, it is stated that the Duke of Norfolk expended £20,000 in keeping Christmas. Charles II. gave over keeping this festival on account, it is said, of its expense. The Duke of Norfolk's profuse hospitality gave great offense at court, where it appears to have been more the fashion to keep disorderly households, than to keep Christmas; and from about the above period of degeneracy, it is said, this good old custom of keeping Christmas began to decline. Indeed it appears that the decline of Christmas customs was really as much owing to the general corruption of manners introduced into England by a profligate king and court, as it was to any influence exercised upon them by the severe Puritanism of Cromwell's time.

The picturesque and poetical custom of bringing in the Yule-log, elsewhere described, though shorn of the "pomp and circumstance" which formerly attended it, is still maintained in various parts of the country. Anciently a Yule song was sung on these occasions. Herrick furnishes an example — written, probably, for the express purpose : —

> "With the last year's brand
> Light the new block, and
> For good success in his spending,
> On your psalteries play
> That sweet luck may
> Come while the log is a-teending" (burning).

Then, it is said, went round the spicy wassail bowl,[1] drowning every former grudge and animosity; an example, it would seem, worthy of modern imitation. "Wassail!" was the word; "Wassail!" every guest returned, as he took the circling goblet from his friend.

---

[1] A fine specimen of a wassail bowl of undoubted Anglo-Saxon work, formerly belonging to the Abbey of Glastonbury, is now in the possession of Lord Arundel of Wardour; it holds two quarts, and formerly had eight pegs inside, dividing the liquor into half pints; on the lid is carved the Crucifixion, with the Virgin and John, one on each side; and round the cup are carved the Twelve Apostles.

The spicy wassail, by the way, besides being sweetened, was also "*augmented*" by the addition of a toast and apples stuck full of cloves; the liquor might be wine, cider, or ale, and was served smoking *hot*.

According to traditional authority, the origin of this wassailing is traced to Rowena, the daughter of the Saxon Hengist. Richard Verstegan (1605) says: —

"As this lady was very beautiful, so was she of a very comely deportment; and Hingistus, having invited King Vortiger to a supper at his new builded castle, caused that after supper she came forth of her chamber into the king's presence, with a cup of gold filled with wine in her hand, and making in very seemly manner a low reverence unto the king, said with a pleasing grace and countenance, 'Waes-heal, hlaford Cyning'—'Be of health, Lord King.'

"Of the beauty of this lady the king took so great liking, that he became exceedingly inamored with her, and desired to have her in marriage, which Hingistus agreed unto, upon condition that the king should give unto him the whole country of Kent, whereunto he willingly condescended, and divorcing himself from his former married wife, married with the Saxon Lady Rowena."

This presentation of the wassail bowl by Rowena, has been thus happily commemorated by a contributor to the "Antiquarian Repertory" (1808): —

"'Health, my lord king,' the sweet Rowena said;
'Health,' cry'd the chieftain, to the Saxon maid;
Then gayly 'rose, and 'midst the concourse wide,
Kiss'd her hale lips, and placed her by his side;
At the soft scene such gentle thoughts abound,
That health and kisses 'mongst the guests went round;
From this the social custom took its rise,
We still retain, and must forever prize."

Perhaps in the "loving cup," still in use in London at the state dinners of the Lord Mayor, there is an allusion to this historical event. The kissing, however, at these civic banquets, is confined to the loving cup or wassail bowl itself, as it circulates from guest to guest; the degenerate Britons of these days being too cautious, it appears, to follow the chivalrous example of the royal Vortiger, who, according to the above cited authority, willingly gave " a kingdom for a kiss."

Bishop Cox, in his " Impressions of England," describing one of these dinners given to the S. P. G. in 1851, says: —

" The toast-master appeared behind his lordship's chair, and began: 'My Lord Archbishop of Canterbury, my Lord Bishop of London,' and so on through the roll of bishops — ' my lords, ladies, and gentlemen, the Lord Mayor and Lady Mayoress greet you in a loving cup and give you a hearty welcome.' The Mayor and Mayoress then rose, and taking the loving cup in hand, she uncovered it for him, with a graceful courtesy, to which he returned a bow, and then drank, wiped the chalice with his napkin, allowed it to be covered, and then sat down, while the lady, turning to the Archbishop, who rose accordingly, repeated the ceremony, save that he uncovered the cup, and it was her turn to taste the draught. Thus the cup went round."

The mystic mistletoe, or kissing-bush, however, appears to have regulated the custom of wassailing at Christmas, for with the disappearance of its white berries, one of which was to be plucked at each kiss, this innocent sport came to an end.

The following imaginary scene from the " Holiday Book," gives us a very good idea of the appearance of one of these old English halls on a Christmas Eve: —

" A fire on the wide hearth-stone ; an oaken table ; with a goodly company ; closed doors ; the mistletoe aloft upon a mighty beam ; evergreens abundant ; the '*Minstrels*' in the tapestried gallery ; quaint figures of '*Mummers*' drolly attired, peep from behind the half-drawn curtains, dependent before the recess of the deep bay-windows."

As an accompaniment to the Yule-log, a candle of monstrous size, called the Yule-candle, or Christmas candle, shed its light on the festive board during the evening. Brand, in his " Popular Antiquities," states that "in the buttery of St. John's College, Oxford, an ancient candle socket of stone still remains, ornamented with the figure of the Holy Lamb. It was formerly used for holding the Christmas candle, which, during the twelve nights of the Christmas festival, was burned on the high table at supper."

CHAPTER V.

CHRISTMAS MUMMERIES.

THE Mysteries, Miracle Plays, and Moralities, formerly enacted during the Christmas holidays, and to which reference has been made in previous chapters, have in modern times gradually disappeared, or degenerated from their pristine splendor and magnificence into mere burlesques, such as the mock play of St. George and the Dragon.

This demoralization, however, does not seem to have extended to the Christmas

Tree, the most picturesque of the mediæval pageants, which, with undiminished glory towering aloft, festooned by garlands of gold and silver paper, and sparkling with its myriad lights, still presents an enchanting vision to thousands of happy children here as well as abroad.

The custom of decorating the Christmas tree, although of German origin and of great antiquity, has but recently been successfully introduced in England and this country. Indeed, it would seem to have been naturalized with us at a much earlier period even than in England. For in Pennsylvania, where many of the settlers are of German descent, Christmas Eve is observed with many of the ceremonies practiced in the Fatherland. The Christmas tree branches forth in all its splendor, and the Christ-Child — according to the German legend — comes flying through the air on golden wings, and causes the bough to produce in the night all manner of fruit, gilt sweetmeats, apples, nuts, etc., for the good children.[1]

It is said that Luther in his family celebrated Christmas Eve according to the German custom. In an engraving published in Leipsic, the great Reformer, who was fond of children and music, is represented

---

[1] Bunsen, it is said, contributed to christianize a heathen custom derived from pagan times, by placing a picture of the Madonna della Seggiola amid the tapers so as to illuminate the loveliest infant representation of Him who brought good gifts unto men; and thus to sanctify the ancient German custom of hanging gifts on a tree, dating from the time of heathen life in a forest. — *Christian Remembrancer*, 1868.

in the midst of both, and playing upon a gittern, an instrument not unlike the modern guitar.

But it is not our well-known Christmas tree and its customs, which it is the especial purpose of the present chapter to notice, but rather those half-forgotten Christmas Mummeries, Plays, and Moralities which once formed the most intellectual part of the sports and pastimes of our ancestors.

The custom of representing at every solemn festival of the church some event recorded in Scripture, became very general in Christendom at an early period.

Gregory Nazianzen, Patriarch of Constantinople, and others eminent in the church, had dramatized portions of the Old and New Testament, and substituted them for the Greek plays still publicly represented in their day.[1] Farces, also, such as the Feast of Fools and of the Ass were enacted, with the design, it is said, of weaning the people from the ancient heathen spectacles, particularly those of the licentious Bacchanalian and Calendary solemnities. The more modern mysteries, miracle plays, and moralities, were also devised by the clergy in later times, doubtless with the same good intention of withdrawing their people at this season of the Nativity from a participation in the traditional games of the Roman Saturnalia.

[1] The sacred dramas of Gregory Nazianzen were modeled on those of the ancient Greek tragedy, the choruses being turned into Christian hymns. One only of the Patriarch's plays, a tragedy called "Christ's Passion," is extant. The Christians found in the wit and elegance of his writings, all that they could desire in the heathen poets.

These were composed of Scriptural incidents, or, as Fitz-Stephen informs us, of "Representations of those miracles that were wrought by holy confessors; or those passions and sufferings in which the martyrs so signally displayed their fortitude. The actors were the scholars of the clergy; the church itself was frequently used as the place of exhibition; and the rich vestments and sacred furniture employed in the church service were sometimes permitted to be used by the performers, to give superior truth and lustre to their representations."

The "*ludi*," or Christmas plays, formerly exhibited at court, were of quite a different character from those described above. It is said they can be traced back certainly as far as the reign of Edward III.; and they are by some thought to be much older. The dresses appropriated in 1348 to one of these plays, show that they were mummeries, and not theatrical divertisements. The King (Edward III.) then kept his Christmas at his castle at Guildford, the "keep" of which remains to this day. The dresses on that occasion, it is said, consisted of eighty tunics of buckram of various colors; forty-two vizors; fourteen faces of women; fourteen of men; and fourteen heads of angels made with silver; twenty-eight crests; fourteen mantles embroidered with heads of dragons; fourteen white tunics, wrought with the heads and wings of peacocks; fourteen with the heads and wings of swans; fourteen tunics, painted with the eyes of peacocks; fourteen tunics of English linen, painted; and fourteen other tunics embroidered with stars of gold.

The magnificent pageants and disguisings frequently exhibited at court, in succeeding reigns, and especially in the reign of Henry VIII., were but a species of mummeries destitute of character and humor; their chief aim being to surprise the spectators "by the ridiculous and exaggerated oddity of the vizors, and by the singularity and splendor of the dresses; — everything was out of nature and propriety."

Stowe thus describes a remarkable mummery made by the citizens of London in 1377, for the disport of the young Prince Richard, son to the Black Prince: —

"They rode, disguised and well horsed, 130 in number, with minstrels and torch-lights of wax, to Kennington beside Lambeth, where the young Prince remained with his mother. These maskers alighted, entered the Palace Hall, and set to the Prince and his mother and lords, cups and rings of gold, which they won at a cast; after which they feasted, and the Prince and lords danced with the mummers, which jollity being ended, they were made to drink," etc.

The plays exhibited in the country at this season appear to have been of a more mixed character. Such were the Cornish mummeries or miracle plays; which were not performed as elsewhere in churches, but in an earthen amphitheatre in some open field. These continued to be exhibited long after the abolition of the miracle plays and moralities in other parts of the kingdom. Accordingly we find them lingering in Cornwall even to the present time; and there, as also in Devonshire and Staffordshire, the old spirit of Christmas is kept up with great earnestness. There is also in the North of England a species of mumming called the sword dance, and, says Mr. Henderson, " this may yet be looked for in most towns from the Humber to the Cheviot Hills." There are some trifling local variations both in dance and song; the latter has altered with the times; the former is plainly a relic of the war dances of our Danish and Saxon ancestors. Tacitus thus describes a sword dance among the ancient Germans: —

" One public diversion was constantly exhibited at all their meetings; young men, who by frequent exercise have attained to great perfection in that pastime, strip themselves, and dance among the points of swords and spears, with most wonderful agility, and even with the most elegant and graceful motions. They do not perform this dance for hire, but for the entertainment of the spectators, esteeming their applause a sufficient reward."

Mr. Brand also tells us that he has seen this dance frequently performed in the North of England, about Christmas, with little or no variation from the ancient method. Washington Irving also refers to the custom in the " Sketch Book." There is a relic of the ancient mystery and miracle plays to be found in the more modern Christmas mummeries; especially in that popular play of " St. George and the Dragon." This is still represented in some parts of England by a sort of dramatic corps headed by " Father Christmas." [1]

[1] See Appendix.

These mummers go abroad and about the country on Christmas Eve, performing this mock play in the halls of the gentry and in the kitchens of farm-houses.

According to the "Golden Legend," on which this old play is founded, the city of Sylene, being infested with a dragon in the marsh, and the sheep failing — which had been given, two a day, to prevent his hurting the people — an ordinance substituted children and young people, to be chosen by lot, whether rich or poor. The king's daughter was drawn, and St. George happening to pass by when she was on her way to be devoured, fought and killed the dragon.

In this legend there seems to be an allusion to the spiritual combat against "that old serpent the Devil," or the "dragon" mentioned in the Apocalypse.

In 1849 this still very popular drama of "St. George and the Dragon" was acted on the floor of the Free Trade Hall in Manchester, where it is customary to celebrate the Epiphany, called Old Christmas or Twelfth Day, with many ancient forms and ceremonies. The programme for each year varies slightly. Sometimes there is a procession of the Months; sometimes of the Seasons, etc.; but there never fail to be the presentation and carrying of the Boar's Head, with the necessary glees and choruses.

Among the religious shows which, like those of the Mysteries and Miracle Plays, gave life and animation to the Christmas festivities of our forefathers, was that of the Boy-Bishop. "The accounts of the origin of this curious custom have been," says Mr. Fosbrooke, "*elucidated* into *obscurity*." It is said to have been founded on this story in the " Legend of St. Nicholas " : —

"A bishop who had been elected to a vacant see, was warned by a dream to go to the doors of the church at the hour of matins, and 'hym that sholde fyrste come to the chyrche, and have the name of Nicholas, they sholde sacre hym Bissop,'— that is, one bishop was superceded by another."— *Gold. Leg.* 29 b.

Hone, on the subject of the Boy-Bishop, writes : —

"Anciently, on the 6th of December (St. Nicholas' Day), the choir-boys in cathedral and collegiate churches chose one of their number to maintain the state and authority of a bishop ; for which purpose he was habited in rich episcopal robes, wore a mitre on his head, and bore a crozier in his hand ; his fellows for the time being assuming the character and dress of priests, yielding him canonical obedience, taking possession of the church, and, except mass, performing all the ceremonies and offices, and on Holy Innocents' Day, actually preaching a sermon to the assembled congregation."

There is a monument of such a child-bishop who died while in office, situated on the north side of Salisbury Cathedral, on which is sculptured the figure of a youth clad in episcopal robes, with his foot on a lion-headed and dragon-tailed monster, in allusion to the expression of the Psalmist, " Thou shalt tread on the lion and the dragon."

Although there resulted much actual profanity from the above prescribed ritualistic observances, yet there seems to have been nothing irreverent intended by them, for we find that whatever was strictly sacramental in its nature, or that properly belonged to the priestly office, was not originally permitted or exercised by these mimic prelates.

"But our ancestors," says Fosbrooke, "used all these mummeries, as we now do the catechism, to impress principles upon the minds of their children."

The election of this "Episcopus Puerorum," or Episcopus *Choristorum*, always took place on St. Nicholas' Day (December 6), and as St. Nicholas was the patron saint of school-boys and choristers, the Boy-Bishop naturally became identified in name with his patron saint. Thus, "St. Nicholas," as he was called, became a person of great consequence, perambulating both town and country, habited as a bishop, "in pontificalibus," with his fellow choristers also in appropriate vestments, singing carols, etc., being in fact Christmas personified, or "Old Father Christmas."

From a printed church-book containing the service of the Boy-Bishop set to music, we learn that on the eve of Innocents' Day, the Boy-Bishop and his youthful clergy, in their copes, and with burning tapers in their hands, went in solemn procession, chanting and singing versicles as they walked, into the choir by the west door, in such order that the dean and canons went foremost, the chaplains next, and the Boy-Bishop, with his priests, in the last and highest place. He then took his seat, and the rest of the children disposed themselves upon each side of the choir, upon the uppermost ascent; the canons *resident* (reversing the usual order) bearing the incense and the book, and the petit-canons the tapers, according to the Rubric. Afterwards he proceeded to the altar of the Holy Trinity and All Saints, which he first censed, and next the Image of the Holy Trinity, his priests all the while singing. Then they all chanted a service with prayers and responses, and, in the like manner taking his seat, the Boy-Bishop repeated salutations, prayers, and versicles; and, in conclusion, gave his benediction to the people, the chorus answering, " Deo Gratias." After he received his crozier from the cross-bearer, other ceremonies were performed, and he chanted the compline; turning toward the choir he delivered an exhortation, and last of all pronounced the benediction.

In process of time, however, all this seemingly orderly behavior was changed for the worse. It appeared that boys would be boys, and that they mixed up with their regularly appointed services the buffooneries of the so-called " Feast of Fools," and of " The Ass," and instead of psalms and hymns, were now " sung or said " indecent songs and jests; and in place of the fragrance of incense, there were substituted all sorts of unsavory abominations.

These enormities had reached such a pitch at the time of the Reformation in the reign of Henry VIII., that we are not surprised to find the ceremonies of the

Boy-Bishop installation abrogated by royal authority. Nevertheless, according to Strype: "In the reacting times of Queen Mary, an edict was issued November 13, 1554, by the Bishop of London, to all the clergy of his diocese, to have the procession of a Boy-Bishop." And again, "On the 5th of December, or St. Nicholas' Eve, of the same year, 'at *even song*,' came a commandment that St. Nicholas should not go abroad or about; but notwithstanding, it seems, so much were the citizens taken with the '*mask*' of St. Nicholas (that is, Boy-Bishop), that there went about these St. Nicholases in divers parishes."

Again, Strype informs us, that "In 1556, on the eve of his day, St. Nicholas, that is, a boy habited like a bishop, 'in pontificalibus,' went abroad in most parts of London, singing after the old fashion, and was received with many ignorant but well-disposed people, into their houses, and had as much good cheer as ever was wont to be had before, at least in many places."

But with the final establishment of the Reformation under Elizabeth, this pastime or pageant of the Boy-Bishop disappears; and henceforth he is not to be found in England, excepting, perhaps, under an alias as "Old Father Christmas."

Ben Jonson appears to have attempted a partial revival of the pageant in his "Masque" presented at court in 1616; in which Christmas is represented in the novel character of an ardent professor of Protestantism. He says: "Ha! would you have kept *me out?*

Christmas, Old Christmas, Christmas of London, and Captaine Christmas! Why, I am no dangerous person, and so I told my friends o' the guard. I am old Gregory Christmas still. And though I come out of Pope's Head Alley, as good a Protestant as any in my Parish."

"Pope's Head Alley" appears to have been intimately related to those celebrated Protestant localities known as Ave Maria Lane, Paternoster Row, and Amen Corner. This plea of his Protestantism, however, did not satisfy the suspicious Puritanical spirit of that age; for at a subsequent period, during the civil wars of the seventeenth century, we find him and his children, mince-pie and plum-porridge included, solemnly banished the land by act of Parliament!

Needham, in his "History of the Rebellion" (1661), bewailing the decline of Christmas, in consequence of Puritanism and of similar legislation, says:—

> "Gone are those golden days of yore,
> When Christmas was a High-Day;
> Whose sports we now shall see no more;
> 'Tis turned into Good-Friday."

But if the Long Parliament could expel him from England, it could not prevent his taking up his abode among the more tolerant Dutch in the "New Netherlands," and where, according to Knickerbocker's "History of New York," "he has continued to flourish at Christmas in spite of the 'Blue Laws' of the neighboring Puritanical State of Connecticut." He does not now, however, go any more abroad, habited " in pontificalibus." Having turned Presbyterian, he contents himself with the ordinary guise of a Dutchman, heavily furred, and has also exchanged his wassail-bowl for the "*bowl*" of a short Dutch pipe, with which he has completely mystified and befogged the intellect of his old enemies, the Puritans.

CHAPTER VI.

CHRISTMAS GAMBOLS.

IN addition to the Christmas mummeries and plays noticed in the preceding chapter, a brief account perhaps should be given of some of the other old English games and amusements appropriate to this season, and especially of the Lord of Misrule, whose authority in some places extended not only over the Christmas holidays, but from the time of his election at Halloween (31st October) even until Whitsuntide.

Brand, in his "Popular Antiquities," speaking of these games, says, "I find in a tract entitled 'Round about our Coal-fire,' or 'Christmas Entertainments,' published in the early part of the last century, the following : —

"Then comes mumming or masquerading, when the squire's wardrobe is ransacked for dresses of all kinds. Corks are burnt to black the faces of the fair, or make deputy mustachios, and every one of the family, except the squire himself, must be transformed."

This account further says : —

"The time of the year being cold and frosty, the diversions are within doors, either in exercise, or by the fireside. Dancing is one of the chief exercises ; or else there is a match at Blindman's Buff or Puss in the Corner. The next game is Questions and Commands, when the commander may oblige his subjects to answer any lawful question, and make the same obey him instantly, under the penalty of being smutted, or paying such forfeit as may be laid on the aggressor. Most of the other diversions are cards and dice."

Although there appears to have been a considerable falling off in modern times in the number and variety of these Christmas games and amusements, still we gather from the above that the sports on a Christmas Eve, a hundred and fifty years ago, were not very much unlike those at present in vogue. The names of almost all the pastimes above mentioned must be familiar to every reader, who has probably participated in some of them. One of these favorite Christmas sports, once generally played on Christmas Eve, has been handed down to us from time immemorial, under the name of Snap-Dragon. In England this amusement is familiar to many people, but as it is not so well known elsewhere, we subjoin from the "Book of Days," a description of the game: —

"A quantity of raisins is deposited in a large bowl or dish (the broader and shallower this is, the better), and brandy or some other spirit is poured over the fruit and ignited. The by-standers now endeavor, by turns, to grasp a raisin, by plunging their hands through the flames; and as this is somewhat of an arduous feat, requiring both courage and rapidity of action, a considerable amount of laughter and merriment is evoked at the expense of the unsuccessful competitors. As an appropriate accompaniment we introduce here —

"THE SONG OF SNAP-DRAGON.

" 'Here he comes with flaming bowl,
Don't he mean to take his toll,
Snip! Snap! Dragon!

" 'Take care you don't take too much,
Be not greedy in your clutch,
Snip! Snap! Dragon!

" 'With his blue and lapping tongue
Many of you will be stung,
Snip! Snap! Dragon!

" 'For he snaps at all that comes
Snatching at his feast of plums,
Snip! Snap! Dragon!

" 'But old Christmas makes him come,
Though he looks so fee! fa! fum!
Snip! Snap! Dragon!

" 'Don't'ee fear him — be but bold —
Out he goes, his flames are cold,
Snip! Snap! Dragon!

"While the sport of Snap-dragon is going on, it is usual to extinguish all the lights in the room, so that the lurid glare from the flaming spirits may exercise to the full its weird-like effect."

Christmas gambols such as these, and indeed holiday festivities of all kinds, were formerly presided over by an officer of great consequence, entitled the "Lord of Misrule, or Christmas Prince." The rights and privileges of this potentate are, it appears, derived from the Roman Saturnalia, a festival instituted in commemoration of the freedom and equality which once prevailed on the earth in the golden reign of Saturn, or, as it has been suggested, from even a still higher origin. For the ancient Jews had among them a sort of Lord of Misrule, or "Symposiarch," as he was called, at their merry-makings, whose duty it was to promote the general hilarity. "If thou be made the master of the feast," says the author of "Ecclesiasticus," "take diligent care for them, and when thou hast done all thy office, take thy place that thou mayest be merry with them, and receive a crown for thy well ordering of the feast."

But whatever may have been the origin of the office, his authority seems to have been pretty generally acknowledged in England previous to the civil wars of the seventeenth century.

A good idea of the merry-makings of our ancestors, and of the nature of the duties of the Lord of Misrule, or master of ceremonies, may be formed from a consideration of the will of the Right Worshipful Richard Evelyn Esqre, of the sixteenth century, father of the author of " The Diary," and Deputy-Lieutenant of the counties of Surrey and Sussex, thus appointing and defining the functions of a Christmas Lord of Misrule, over his estate at Wotton : —

"*Imprimis.* — I give free leave to Owen Flood, my trumpeter, gentleman, to be Lord of Misrule of all good orders during the twelve days. And also I give free leave to the said Owen Flood, to command all and every person or persons whatsoever, as well servants as others, to be at his command whensoever he shall sound his trumpet or music, and to do him service, as though I were present myself, at their perils. . . . . I give full power and authority to his lordship to break up all locks, bolts, bars, doors, and latches, and to fling up all doors out of hinges, to come at those who presume to disobey his lordship's commands. God save the king ! "

Sir Richard's son did not depart from the economy and hospitality of the old house, but "*more veterum,*" kept a Christmas in which they had not fewer than three hundred bumpkins every holiday.

Hollingshed also informs us that —

" What time there is alwayes one appointed to make sporte at Courte, called commonly, Lord of Misrule, whose office is not unknowne to such as have been brought up in nobleman's houses, and among great housekeepers, which use liberal feasting in the season."

Again, Stowe says, —

" At the Feast of Christmas, in the king's court, wherever he chanced to reside, there was appointed a Lord of Misrule, or master of merry disports ; the same merry-fellow made his appearance at the house of every nobleman and person of distinction, and among the rest the Lord Mayor of London, and the sheriffs, had severally of them their Lord of Misrule ; ever contending, without quarrel or offense, who should make the rarest pastimes to delight the beholders ; this pageant potentate began his rule at All-hallow Eve, and continued the same till the morrow after the Feast of the Purification, in which space there were fine and subtle disguisings, masks, and mummeries."

The sway of this officer, the Master of Merry Disports, was not confined to the court, nor to the houses of the opulent; but he was also elected in various towns and parishes, where, however, his reign seems to have been of shorter duration.

The practical result of this facetious and popular species of misrule perhaps may be gathered in part from the graphic description left by Stubbs, who, from all accounts, was himself a notable rebel not only against "*misrule*," but also against all "right rule." In the "Anatomy of Abuses," he says : —

"First of all, the wilde heads of the parish flocking togither, chuse them a graund captaine of mischiefe, whom they innoble with the title of Lord of Misrule ; and him they crowne with great solemnity, and adopt for their king. This king annoynted chooseth forth twentie, fourty, threescore, or an hundred, lustie guttes, like to himself, to waite upon his lordly majesty, and to guarde his noble person. Then every one of these men he investeth with his liveries of greene, yellow, or some other light wanton colour, and as though they were not gaudy ynaugh, they bedecke themselves with scarffes, ribbons and laces, hanged all over with gold ringes, pretious stones, and other jewels. This done, they tie about either legge twentie, or fourtie belles, with rich handkerchiefes in their handes, and sometimes laide across over their shoulders and neckes, borrowed, for the most part, of their pretie Mopsies and loving Bessies. Thus all thinges set in order, then have they their *hobby*-horses, their dragons, and other antiques, together with their baudie pipers, and thundring drummers to strike up the devils daunce withal. Then march this heathen company towards the church, their pypers pyping, their drummers thundring, their stumpes dauncing, their belles jyngling, their handkerchiefes fluttering aboute their heades like madde men, their *hobby*-horses and other monsters skirmishing amongst the throng : and in this state they go to the church though the minister be at prayer or preaching, dauncing and singing like devils incarnate, with such a confused noise that no man can heare his owne voyce. Then the foolish people they looke, they stare, they laugh, they fleere, and mount upon the formes and pewes, to see these goodly pageants solemnized. Then after this, aboute the church they go againe and againe, and so fourthe into the churche-yard, where they have commonly their summer halls, their bowers, arbours, and banqueting houses set up, wherein they feaste, banquette, and daunce all that day, and peradventure all that night too ; and thus these terrestrial furies spend the Sabbath-day. Then, for the further innobling of this honourable lordane — lord I should say — they have certaine papers wherein is painted some babelerie or other of imagerie worke, and these they call my Lord of Misrules badges or cognizances. These they give to every one that will give them money to mantaine them in this their heathenish devilrie ; and who will not show himself buxome to them and give them money, they shall be mocked and flouted shamefully ; yea, and many times carried upon a cowlstaffe, and dived over heade and eares in water, or otherwise most horribly abused. And so besotted are some, that they not only give them money, but weare their badges or cognizances in their hattes or cappes openly. Another sorte of fantasticall fooles bring to these hell-hounds, the Lord of Misrule and his com-

plices, some bread, some good ale, some new cheese, some old cheese, some custardes, some cracknels, some cakes, some flauns, some tartes, some creame, some meate, some one thing and some another."

It would seem from the above, although Strutt appears to have inferred in his "Sports and Pastimes" that Stubbs was speaking of the Christmas holidays, that the Lord of Misrule was sometimes also president over the summer sports; and that his authority appears to have been occasionally extended over the whole period, from All-hallows till Whitsuntide. Stubbs speaks of this revel being on the Sabbath-day, and also of their erecting summer-halls, etc., in the church-yard, from which we may infer that the Sabbath-day mentioned, was a *Whitsunday*, because, the "belles that were tied about either legge," indicate the morris-dance, a dance peculiar to Whitsuntide.

But the amusing account by Stubbs of the Lord of Misrule, and his alleged evil doings, does not convey to us so truthful an impression of this mighty potentate, as may be derived from other less prejudiced sources.

In contrast with the above, we subjoin an account of certain stately proceedings by the lawyers of the Inner Temple. In 1561, a Lord of Misrule, having with him a train of one hundred horsemen, richly appareled, rode through London to the Inner Temple, where there was great reveling throughout the Christmas. Lord Robert Dudley, afterwards Earl of Leicester, being the constable and marshal, under the name of Palaphilos, and Christopher Hatton, afterwards Chancellor, master of the game. A sort of Parliament had been previously held on St. Thomas's Eve, to decide whether the society should keep Christmas, and if so, the oldest bencher should deliver a speech on the occasion, and the oldest butler publish the officers' names, and then — " in token of joy and good liking, the bench and company pass beneath the hearth, and sing a carol, and so to *boyer* " (collation).

Again, in 1629, we read that —

"The Templars chose Bulstrode Whitelocke as Master of the Revels; and as soon as the evening was come, entered the hall followed by sixteen revellers. They were proper handsome young gentlemen, habited in rich suits, shoes and stockings, hats and great feathers. The Master led them in his bar gown, with a white staff in his hand, the music playing before them. They began with the old masques; after which they daunced the *Brawls*, and then the Master took his seat, while the revellers flaunted through galliards, corantos, French and country dances, till it grew very late. As might be expected, the reputation of this dancing soon brought a store of other gentlemen and ladies, some of whom were of great quality. To crown the ambition and vanity of all, a great German lord had a desire to witness the revels, then making such a sensation at court, and the Templars entertained him at great cost to themselves, receiving in exchange that which cost the great noble very little, — his avowal that 'Dere was no such nople gollege in Ghristendom as deirs.'"

The Templars, according to Hone, also formerly held in their hall at Christmas, around about their coal fire, a species of hunt with hound and horn, conducted by the Lord of Misrule; a fox and cat being the game pursued. This hunt seems at one time to have been general in great houses, and to have had a sort of symbolic signification. What that was before the Reformation, does not appear, but "In ane compendious Boke of godly and spiritual Songs, Edinburgh, 1621, printed from an old copy," are the following lines, seemingly referring to some such pageant:—

> "The hunter is Christ that hunts in haist,
> The hunds are Peter and Pawle,
> The Paip is the fox, Rome is the rox,
> That rubbis us on the gall."

There was also, it appears, a very splendid Christmas at the Middle Temple in 1635, when Mr. Francis Vivian of Cornwall was the Christmas Prince, and expended £2,000 out of his own pocket, beyond the allowance of the society, in order to support his state with sufficient dignity. He had his lord keeper, lord treasurer, eight white staves, captain of pensioners, and his guard, and two chaplains, who, when they preached before him, saluted him on ascending the pulpit, with three low bows, as was then done to the king.[1]

---

[1] Sandys says: "Towards the end of the seventeenth century these revels ceased, having gradually fallen off; and the dignity of Master of the Revels instead of being eagerly sought for, as in former times, required a bribe or premium to induce any member to take it upon him."

But the sad and sober days of the Commonwealth came, and brought with them an end (as of many better things) of this species of high misrule. For in these gloomy days the Long Parliament, it appears, disgusted the nation, turning jest into earnest, by choosing at Westminster the " Lord Protector " Cromwell to be their Lord of Misrule."

CHAPTER VII.

THE CHRISTMAS BANQUETS OF THE OLDEN TIME.

THE custom of serving the boar's head with minstrelsy at the Christmas dinner, with more or less of the ceremonies still used at Queen's College, Oxford, was very general in England previous to the civil wars of the seventeenth century, not only in the halls of the Universities, but also in the houses of the nobility and gentry. According to Aubrey,—"The first dish that was served up in the old baronial halls, was the boar's head, which was brought in with great state, and with minstrelsy; and between the flourishes of the heralds' trumpets, carols were chanted forth."

Perhaps the most splendid example of Christmas banqueting of this kind of which we have read, is that recently illustrated by Gilbert, which took place in the reign of Henry VII., in the great hall of Westminster. To this feast the Mayor and Aldermen of London were invited, and all the sports of the time were exhibited before them in the great hall, which was hung with tapestry; "which sports being ended *in the morning*, the King, Queen, and Court sat down at a table of stone, to one hundred and twenty dishes, placed by as many knights and esquires; while the Mayor was served with twenty-four dishes and abundance of wine. And finally, the King and Queen being conveyed with great lights into the palace, the Mayor with his company, in barges, returned to London by break of next day."

It is this royal Christmas which Mr. Gilbert has represented with such truthfulness. The artist has selected the upper end of the hall, showing the great stone table, with the King and Queen seated beneath a canopy of state, emblazoned with the royal arms; the dais wall is hung with tapestry, and wreathed with Christmas evergreens, and the banners above are surmounted with laurel crowns. The servitors are bringing in the royal dishes, conspicuous amongst which

is the peacock in all its glory of gaudy plumage, and the boar's head dressed with holly, bay, and rosemary.

Another celebrated account of a Christmas dinner, at the time of the famous "Christmas Prince" (or Lord of Misrule) who presided over the festivities at St. John's, Oxford, in 1607, is given us by Aubrey:—

"The first messe was a boar's head, wch was carried by the tallest and lustiest of all ye guard, before whom (as attendants) wente first, one attired in a horseman's coate, wth a boar's spear in his hande; next to him another huntsman in greene wth a bloody faulcion drawne; next to him 2 pages in tafatye sarcenet, each of y^{em} wth a messe of mustard; next to whome came hee that carried ye boar's head crost wth a greene silke scarfe, by wch hunge ye empty scabbard of the faulcion wch was carried before him. As y^{ei} entered ye hall, he sange this Christmas Caroll ye three last verses of eurie staffe being repeated after him by the whole companye."

The ceremony *now* observed in Queen's College, Oxford, differs but little from the above. Brawn,[1] decorated with bay and rosemary, has been substituted for the boar's head, but otherwise the dish is brought in with very much of the same state and ceremony, the choir in their surplices singing in procession, by *way of grace*, the Carol —

---

[1] The following traditional receipt we give as we had it from an English lady. "*Brawn.*— Take a pig's head and soak in salt and water all night, scrape and well clean the head, removing the brains and eyes. Boil until tender enough to take the bones out easily. When quite tender pick the meat from the bones and chop fine, seasoning to your taste, with red and black pepper, cloves, mace, nutmeg, and salt; mix well together and put in a press. Let it remain until cold."

> "Caput apri defero
> Reddens laudes, Domino."

Various accounts have been given of the origin of this ancient custom. By some it is said to have originated with the Romans, who were accustomed to serve up the wild boar, sometimes in parts, sometimes the animal, as the first dish at their feasts.

The boar's head was also an established Yule-tide dish of the North in the old heathen times. The whole boar and boar's head, gorgeously ornamented, gilt, and painted, was also a favorite festival dish in England during the Norman era. Perhaps, as the wild boar was anciently accounted a public enemy, ferocious and destructive, a successful encounter with him was in those days considered an achievement worthy the valor of an accomplished knight, entitling him to the gratitude of the country. An old carol from Mr. Wright's MS. seems to confirm this supposition: —

> "Tidings I bring you for to tell
> What in wild forest me befell,
> When I in with a wild beast fell,
> With a boar so bryme" (fierce).

> "A boar so bryme that me pursued,
> Me for to kill so sharply moved,
> That brymly beast so cruel and rude,
>   There tamed I him,
> And reft from him both life and limb.

"Truly, to show you this is true,
 His head I with my sword did hew,
 To make this day new mirth for you,
   Now eat thereof anon.

"Eat, and much good do it you,
 Take your bread and mustard thereto;
 Joy with me, that this I have done,
 I pray you be glad every one,
   And all rejoice as one."

The curious custom called the "Rhyne Toll of Chetwode Manor," may be also cited by way of illustration. The tradition is, that at a very early period of English history, a lord of Chetwode, the ancestor of the present proprietor, slew in single combat an enormous wild boar, the terror of the surrounding country. For this good service, he and his heirs had conferred on them by royal authority certain valuable manorial rights and privileges, which the family enjoy to this day. An old ballad modernized thus commemorates the deed: —

"Then he blowed a blast full North, South, East, and West —
   Wind well thy horn good hunter! —
 And the wild boar then heard him full in his den,
   As he was a jovial hunter.

"Then he made the best of his speed unto him —
   Wind well thy horn good hunter! —
 Swift flew the boar, with his tusks smear'd with gore,
   To Sir Ryalas, the jovial hunter.

"Then the wild boar, being so stout and strong —
   Wind well thy horn good hunter! —
Thrash'd down the trees as he ramped him along,
   To Sir Ryalas, the jovial hunter.

Then they fought four hours in a long summer day.—
   Wind well thy horn good hunter! —
Till the wild boar fain would have got him away
   From Sir Ryalas, the jovial hunter.

"When Sir Ryalas he drawed his broadsword with might-
   Wind well thy horn good hunter! —
And he fairly cut the boar's head off quite,
   For he was a jovial hunter."

This tradition (thus commemorated) received, about half a century since, a remarkable confirmation. Within a mile of Chetwode Manor house there existed a large mound, surrounded by a ditch, and bearing the name of the "Boar's Pond." About the year 1810, the tenant to whose farm it belonged, wishing to bring it into cultivation, began to fill up the ditch by leveling the mound, when having lowered the latter about four feet, he came on the skeleton of an enormous boar, lying flat on its side, and at full length. The field containing it is still called the Boar's Head Field.[1]

There is, however, a very different account of the origin of the custom of serving the boar's head at Christmas, given by Dean Wade, in his "Walks about Oxford": —

[1] See Chambers' *Book of Days*.

"Tradition presents this usage as a commemoration of an act of valor, performed by a student of a college, who, walking in the neighboring forest of Shotover, and reading 'Aristotle,' was suddenly attacked by a wild boar. The furious beast came open-mouthed upon the youth, who, however, very courageously and with a happy presence of mind, is said to have rammed in the volume and cried, '*Græcum est*' (it is Greek); fairly," adds the Dean, "choking the savage with the sage."

Perhaps this manner of disposing of two enemies at once was considered by the Oxonians of that day an event worthy of a particular commemoration; the Greek philosopher, in their estimation, being the most dreadful *bore* of the two. But whether or not the modern philosophy which succeeded that of Aristotle in this University derived its name "Baconian" from this combat, has not, it appears, been yet decided. Possibly the youth mentioned by the Dean may have acquired the surname of "Bacon" from this exploit, and so transmitted it to posterity with the "inductive" or "Baconian system." The crest of Lord Bacon — the wild boar passant — with the motto "*mediocria firma*" seems to indicate something of the kind.

The places where *now* the boar's head ceremony is specially observed, by bringing in the gigantic dish in procession, with song and chorus, on Christmas Day, are Queen's College, Oxford; St. John's College, Cambridge; and the Inner Temple, London.

There has been also elsewhere, and even in this country, a successful attempt at a revival of this ancient ceremony, especially at the Twelfth Night parties of the "Century Club" in New York, where the boar's head is annually served at the supper in this manner.[1]

But to return to the subject (the Christmas of our forefathers), the banquet would have been thought very incomplete without the appearance of the Christmas-pie, which was also anciently served with minstrelsy, but without the carol, the peculiar honor reserved for the boar's head — that "chiefest dish in all the land."

This Christmas-pie was, it appears, quite a bill of fare in itself. Indeed, fish, flesh, and fowl were to be found beneath its ample crust. We read that, — " In the 26th Henry III., the Sheriff of Gloucester was ordered by that monarch to procure twenty salmon to be put into pies at Christmas; and the Sheriff of Sussex, ten brawns, ten peacocks, and other items for the same purpose." The peacock was only produced at solemn and chivalric banquets, such as that of Christmas, and when thus served up, with gilded beak and plumed crest, his head appearing at one end of the

---

[1] In 1865, at a Christmas dinner in the school-room attached to the Church of the Holy Cross, Troy, N. Y., the boar's head was thus served with minstrelsy, the choir of the Church singing in procession the appropriate carol; the first bass, with his hand on the silver dish, chanting the solo : —

"The boar's head in hand bear I,
Bedecked with bay and rosemary."

The school-room on the occasion presented quite the appearance of an antique baronial hall, with its arched fire-place and blazing Yule-log.

pie, and his tail at the other, spread out in all its glory, was carried in state into the hall to the sound of minstrelsy, by the lady most distinguished for birth and beauty, the other ladies following in due order.

Some of the dishes of the olden time do not appear to us to be very inviting; yet others have stood the test of ages, as we see in the instance of a Christmas-pie, the receipt to make which is preserved in the books of the Salters' Company, in London: —

"For to make a moost choyce Paaste of Gamys to be eten at ye Feste of Chrystemasse (17th Richard II. A. D. 1394)."

A pie so made by the Company's cook in 1836, was found excellent. It consisted of a pheasant, hare, and capon; two partridges, two pigeons, and two rabbits; all boned and put into paste in the shape of a bird, with the livers and hearts, two mutton kidneys, forcemeats, and egg-balls, seasoning, spice, catsup, and pickled mushrooms, filled up with gravy made from the various bones.

The North of England in more modern times continued to maintain a reputation for its Christmas-pies, composed of birds and game. In the "Newcastle Chronicle" of January 6, 1770, there is a description of a giant of this race: —

"On Monday last was brought from Howick to Berwick, to be shipped for London, for Sir Henry Grey, Bart., a pie, the contents whereof are as follows, viz.: 2 bushels of flour, 20 lbs. of butter, 4 geese, 2 turkies, 2 rabbits, 4 wild ducks, 2 woodcocks, 6 snipes, and 4 partridges, 2 neats' tongues, 2 curlews, 7 blackbirds, and 6 pigeons. It is supposed this very great curiosity was made by Mrs. Dorothy Patterson, housekeeper at Howick. It is near nine feet in circumference at bottom, weighs about 12 stone ; will take two men to present it to table ; it is neatly fitted with a case and four small wheels to facilitate its use to every guest that inclines to partake of its contents at table."

The learned Dr. Parr says of the mince-pie, which under its changed name continues to maintain its celebrity, that it should more properly be called *The Christmas-pie*, the term *mince* having been given to it in derision by the Puritans; indeed, in the seventeenth century, the eating of this pie became a test of orthodoxy. Bunyan, when in confinement and in distress for a comfortable meal, is said to have refused to injure his morals by eating it, the Puritans of his day holding it to be a superstitious abomination. For —

> "The high-shoe lords of Cromwell's making
> Were not for dainties — roasting, baking ;
> The chiefest food they found most good in
> Was rusty bacon and bag-pudding ;
> Plum-broth was 'Popish,' and mince-pie —
> O, that was flat idolatry !" —
>
> *Poor Robin's Almanack*, 1685.

Anciently this pie was baked in the form of a *crache* or *manger*, the crossed bands at the top being traditionally considered to resemble the manner in which a child is secured in its crib. Its various savory contents had, it is supposed, some reference to the offerings of the Magi.

There is a superstition in regard to these pies worthy of notice. It is said that in as many different houses as you eat *mince-pie* during Christmas, so many happy months will you have during the ensuing year. Now, as there are just twelve days of Christmas, an enterprising diner-out may thus secure twelve happy months for the New Year.

CHAPTER VIII.

TWELFTH-DAY, OR OLD CHRISTMAS.[1]

N the primitive Church the Feast of the Nativity appears to have been observed by the Eastern and Western Churches on different days. The Oriental Church keeping it on the 6th of January, calling it the Epiphany,[1] and the Western Church, from the earliest

---

[1] According to the change of the style (made in England by act of Parliament, 1752), "Old Christmas Day," as it is called, in contradistinction to that of the

time, on the 25th of December. Bingham says that this day was kept as our Saviour's birthday for several ages by the churches of Egypt, Jerusalem, Antioch, Cyprus, and other churches of the East. In the fourth century, Chrysostom, in one of his homilies to the people of Antioch, tells them that — " Ten years were not yet passed since they came to the true knowledge of the day of Christ's birth, which they kept before on Epiphany, till the Western Church gave them better information." From that time it appears that the Nativity and Epiphany were kept as distinct festivals. Both Cassian and Jerome say: —

" The Nativity and Epiphany were kept on different days in all the Western Churches, and both these were indifferently called *Theophania et Epiphania, et prima et secunda Nativitas*, — the 'Epiphany' or 'Manifestation of God,' and his first and second Nativity; that being the first, whereon he was born in the flesh, and that his second Nativity, or Epiphany, whereon he was baptized, and manifested by a star to the Gentiles."

In the fourth century, however, the Easterns changed their festival of the Nativity, and united with the Westerns in observing the 25th of December. This variation in the early usage of the Greek and Latin Churches may have originated the custom of observing twelve days as the Christmas holidays.

The Epiphany is said to denote Christ's manifesta-

new style, falls on the Eve of Epiphany or Twelfth-Day, and in some places, says Mr. Hone, " is still observed as the festival of the Nativity."

tion to the world in four several respects, which at first were all commemorated upon this day, namely: (1.) By his Nativity or Incarnation. (2.) By the appearance of the Star which guided the Wise Men unto Christ at his birth. (3.) By the glorious appearance that was made at his baptism. (4.) By the manifestation of his Divinity, when by his first miracle He turned the water into wine, at the marriage of Cana in Galilee.

In England the twelve days of Christmas were certainly observed as early as the time of Alfred the Great, and probably from a much earlier period. Collier, in his "Ecclesiastical History of Britain," cites a law of Alfred in which, "the twelve days after the Nativity of our Saviour are made holy days."

The Magi, or "Wise Men of the East," commemorated at the Epiphany, are supposed to have been Persians. These Magi in their own country were philosophers or priests, and besides were sometimes royal counselors, physicians, astrologers, or mathematicians. In fact they were similar to the Brahmins of India, the Philosophers among the Greeks, and the Druids among the Gauls. Zoroaster, one of their number and King of Bactria, the great reformer of the sect of the Magi, has left on record a curious prophecy relating to the future birth of a Saviour, and its announcement by a Star, which seems to agree in a remarkable manner with that of Balaam: "There shall come a Star out of Jacob, and a Sceptre shall rise out of Israel." Says Abul Pharajius, speaking of Zoroaster, —

"He taught the Persians the manifestation of the Lord Christ, commanding that they should bring him gifts; and revealed to them that it would happen in the latter time that a virgin would conceive without contact with a man, and that when her child was born, a star would appear and shine by day, in the midst of which would be seen the figure of a virgin. ' But you, my children, will see its rising before all the nations. When, therefore, ye shall behold it, go whither the star shall guide ye and adore the child, and offer up to him your gifts, seeing that he is the Word, which has created the Heavens.'"

Blunt says : —

"Some authors have suggested, and it seems not improbable, that the '*Star*' which appeared to the Wise Men in the East might be that glorious light which shone upon the Shepherds of Bethlehem, when the angels came to give them the glad tidings of our Saviour's birth. According to an ancient commentary on St. Matthew, this Star, on its first appearance to the Magi, had the form of a radiant child bearing a sceptre or cross ; and in some early Italian frescoes, it is so depicted."

The Wise Men who came to Jerusalem in the days of Herod, are traditionally believed to have been three in number, and of the rank of kings or princes. The Venerable Bede, in the seventh century, was the first writer in England who gave a description of them, which he is supposed to have taken from some earlier account. According to Bede. —

"Melchior was old, with gray hair and long beard, and offered gold to our Saviour in acknowledgment of his sovereignty ; Jaspar was young, without any beard, and offered frankincense in recognition of the Divinity; and Balthasar was of a dark complexion as a Moor, with a large spreading beard, and offered myrrh to our Saviour's humanity."

The tradition is that they were baptized by St. Thomas, and afterwards themselves preached the gospel. In the fourth century their bodies were said to have been discovered by the Empress Helena, and taken to Constantinople; from thence to Milan; and when that city was taken by the Emperor Frederick in 1164, he gave these relics to Reinaldus, Archbishop of Cologne, whence they are commonly called "The Three Kings of Cologne."

In England, a striking memorial of the offerings of the Magi is kept up by the sovereigns, who make an oblation of gold, frankincense, and myrrh, at the Altar of the Chapel Royal in the Palace of St. James, on this festival.

The story of the Three Kings of Cologne forms the subject of many of the early "mysteries," formerly so popular. There are, indeed, said to have been representations of the Magi in the French churches as early as the fifth century, and there are French mysteries relating to them in the eleventh century, and also a Latin one, wherein Virgil (who appears to have usually taken a conspicuous part in mediæval pageantry, and was supposed to have been a magician), accompanies the kings on their journey, and at the end of the adoration joins them very devoutly in the "benedicamus."

The Adoration of the Magi was a favorite subject in our early English mysteries. In " Dives and Pauper," 1496, we read : " For to represente in playnge at Crystmasse Herodes and the Thre Kynges and other processes of the gospelles both than and at Ester, and at other times also, it is befull and comendable."

These mysteries were suppressed early in the time of James the First; but the Adoration of the Magi was afterwards introduced as a puppet show at Bartholomew Fair, as late as the time of Queen Anne.

This representation of the Adoration of the Magi has given place in more modern times, at least in France and England, to the still popular game of drawing for king and queen on Twelfth-Night. This custom has generally been supposed to be in honor of the Three Kings of Cologne; although Mr. Soane thinks that in all probability it owes its origin to a Greek and Roman custom of casting lots at their banquets for who should be the "*Rex Convivii*," or as Horace calls him, the "*Arbiter Bibendi*."[1] However, this custom, according to Strutt, "was a common Christmas gambol in both of the English universities, previous to the beginning of the last century."

An old calendar says: " On the 5th of January —

---

[1] " After the rose and ivy wreaths and perfumes and ointments had been distributed, the chairman or king of the feast was chosen by throw of dice. He who threw Venus, or the six, became king. The lowest cast was called the dog." — *The Albion.*

the Vigil of the Epiphany — the Kings of the Bean are created, and on the 6th the feast of the Kings shall be held, and also of the Queen, and let the banqueting be continued for many days."

The usage now in regard to this game — particularly in France and England — is to place a bean and pea (or ring) in a Twelfth-cake, which, being divided, is distributed, and the persons finding the bean and pea, are the King and Queen of Twelfth-Night.

Two hundred years ago the ingredients of the bean-cake were flour, honey, ginger, and pepper. "But it would not compete," says Mr. Sandys, ' with that beautiful, frosted, festooned, bedizened, and ornamented piece of confectionery, now called, *par eminence*, 'Twelfth-cake,' with its splendid waxen or plaster-of-paris kings and queens, the delight and admiration of school-boys and girls."

In some parts of France the Bean-King is elected by another process. A child is placed under a table where he can see nothing; and the master of the feast, holding up a piece of cake, demands whose portion it is to be. The child replies according to his own fancy, and this game continues till the piece which contains the bean has been allotted. A whole court is thus formed, the *fool* not being forgotten, and every time either of these magistrates is seen to drink, the company are bound to cry out under pain of forfeit, " The King (or the Queen) drinks."

Before concluding it should be mentioned that during the whole of the twelve days of Christmas, most of the social usages and observances noticed in the preceding chapters were continued with more or less variation. The Yule-log and Christmas-candle were burnt until Twelfth-Night. A small portion of the old log was carefully preserved to light that of the following year, and on the last day of its being in use, which in some places was even as late as Candlemas-Day (February 2), which festival in popular estimation was the conclusion of the Christmas holidays, a small piece of the Christmas block having been kept on purpose, the practice was, to —

> "Kindle the Christmas brand, and then
> Till sunset let it burne;
> Which quenched, then lay it up agen,
> Till Christmas next returne.
>
> "Part must be kept, wherewith to teend
> The Christmas log next yeare;
> And where it is safely kept, the fiend
> Can do no mischief there."

There are many other curious superstitions connected with the burning of the Yule-log. It is said the maidens that blow a Christmas fire should be like suitors in a law court, and come to the task with clean hands: —

> "Wash your hands, or else the fire
> Will not teend to your desire;

>   Unwashed hands, ye maidens know,
>   Dead the fire though ye blow."

Moreover no person that squints should be permitted to enter the room when it is lit on Christmas Eve; nor should any one barefooted be allowed to pass through the hall. In France the Yule-log was once believed to keep away pestilence from all who were seated around it, this protection extending throughout the year.

>   "Now, now the mirth comes
>   With the cake full of plums,
>   Where Bean's the King of the sports here;
>   Besides we must know,
>   The Pea also,
>   Must revel as Queen in the court here.
>
>   "Begin then to choose,
>   This night as you use,
>   Who shall, for the present delight here,
>   Be a King by the lot,
>   And who shall not
>   Be Twelfth-Day Queen for the night here.
>
>   "Next crown the bowl full
>   With gentle lamb's wool;[1]

---

[1] Until recently at least "lamb's wool" was a customary beverage at Christmas in the Southern States, although rum and water were used for lack of ale.

The old compound of roasted apples, ale, and sugar, which our ancestors knew as "lamb's wool," is thought, says the author of "Nooks and Corners of English Life," to have derived its name as follows: "The words La Mas Ubal

Add sugar, nutmeg, and ginger,
  With store of ale too;
And thus must ye do,
To make the wassail a swinger!

"Give then to the King
  And Queen wassailing;
And though with ale ye be wet here,
  Yet part ye from hence,
  As free from offense,
As when ye innocent met here." — *Herrick*.

are good Irish, signifying the feast or day of the apple, and pronounced *Lamasool*, soon passed into 'Lamb's Wool.'"

CHAPTER IX.

SHROVE-TIDE, OR CARNIVAL.

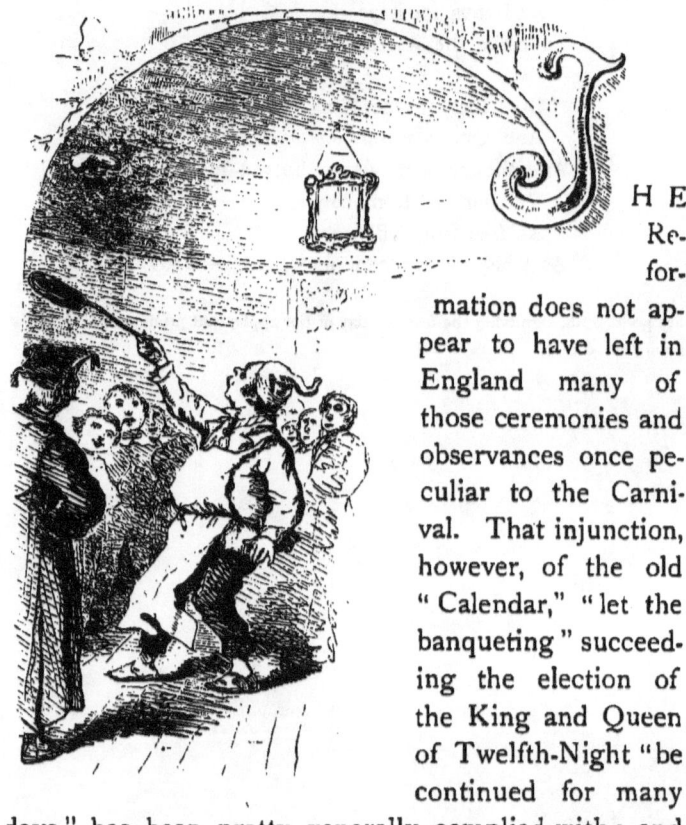

THE Reformation does not appear to have left in England many of those ceremonies and observances once peculiar to the Carnival. That injunction, however, of the old "Calendar," "let the banqueting" succeeding the election of the King and Queen of Twelfth-Night "be continued for many days," has been pretty generally complied with; and

Shrove-tide, or the Carnival, still continues to usher in the sombre season of Lent with extraordinary gayety.

Taylor, the Water Poet, in his "Jack-a-Lent" works, 1630, gives the following curious account of the Shrove-Tuesday observances of his time: —

"Shrove-Tuesday at whose entrance in the morning all the whole kingdom is in quiet, but by that time the clock strikes eleven, which (by the help of a knavish sexton) is commonly before nine, then there is a bell rung, cal'd the Pancake-bell, the sound whereof makes thousands of people distracted, and forgetfull either of manners or humanitie; then there is a thing cald wheaten flowre, which the cookes doe mingle with water, egges, spice, and other tragicall, magicall inchantments, and then they put it by little into a frying-pan of boyling suet, where it makes a confused dismall hissing (like the Learnean snakes in the reeds of Acheron, Stix or Phlegethon) untill, at last, by the skill of the cooke, it is transferred into the form of a Flap-jack, cal'd a Pancake, which ominous incantation the ignorant people doe devoure very greedily."

This Pancake-bell, which in ancient times called the faithful to confession, still continues in some places to summon people to the more cheerful occupation above described.

According to the "Book of Days," this custom is still observed with great solemnity at the Westminster School: —

"At 11 o'clock, A. M., a verger of the Abbey, in his gown, bearing a silver mace, emerges from the college kitchen, followed by the cook of the school, in his white apron, jacket, and cap, and carrying a pancake. On arriving at the school-room door, he announces himself 'The Cook;' and having entered the school-room, he advances to the bar which separates the upper school from the lower one, twirls the pancake in the pan, and then tosses it over the bar into the upper school, among a crowd of boys who scramble for the pancake; and he who gets it unbroken, and carries it to the Deanery, demands the honorarium of a guinea (sometimes two guineas) from the Abbey funds; though the custom is not mentioned in the Abbey Statutes. The cook also receives two guineas for his performance."

But besides such curious *pancake* ceremonies as these, there were also other observances peculiar to the season, some of which have survived not only the period of the Reformation, but even the "No Popery" cry that succeeded it.

But before referring to these it might be well to notice the custom of going a mothering on Mid-Lent Sunday—a social festivity connected with those of the Carnival. Durandus says: "The faithful who might be supposed to be worn out by the long fast, were now to indulge themselves, for it was a season which the Church allowed and wished to be one of general enjoyment."

The result of this ecclesiastical indulgence was a revival, particularly on the Continent, of many of the Carnival observances, which had only been suspended.

The English, however, contented themselves, at least since the Reformation, with going a "mothering" on Mid-Lent Sunday. This practice is derived from the ancient custom of the people making pilgrimages to their cathedral or "Mother Church," and making their offerings at the high altar.

The term "*mothering*" is supposed to be derived from the Epistle for the day (Gal. iv. 21), "Jerusalem mater omnium"—Jerusalem is the mother of us all. Both the Epistle and Gospel are still retained in the "Book of Common Prayer."

Associated with this observance was the similar custom of children visiting their parents and making presents to them, especially to their mothers, the offering being usually a simnel loaf, a commemoration of the miraculous feeding of the multitude mentioned in the Gospel for the day.

Herrick, referring to this custom in a canzonet, says: —

"I'll to thee a simnel bring,
'Gainst thou go a mothering;
So that when she blesses thee,
Half that blessing thou'lt give me."

The simnel loaf alluded to was a rich and expensive raised cake, the crust of which is made of fine flour and water, with sufficient saffron to give it a deep yellow color; and the interior is filled with the materials of a very rich plum cake, with plenty of candied lemon peel and other good things. It is made up very stiff, tied up in a cloth, and boiled for several hours, after which it is brushed over with egg, and then baked.

Ducange says that it was usual in early times to make the simnels with the figure of Christ, or of the Virgin Mary, which is a proof that they once had, as has been suggested, a religious signification. The mothering cakes are now very highly ornamented, artists being employed to paint them. A mothering cake is thus alluded to in " Collins' Miscellanies " : —

> " Why, rot thee, Dick, see Dundry's Peak
> Lucks like a shuggar'd motherin' cake."

It is an old custom still maintained in Shropshire and Herefordshire, and especially at Shrewsbury, for shopkeepers to manufacture and sell these simnel loaves during Lent and Easter, and also at Christmas.

But to return. At Shrove-tide the favorite amusement was the game of foot-ball. Brand says : —

> " With regard to the custom of playing at foot-ball on Shrove-Tuesday, I was informed that at Alnwick Castle in Northumberland, the waits belonging to the town came playing to the castle every year on Shrove-Tuesday, at two o'clock, P. M., when a foot-ball was thrown over the castle walls to the populace. I saw this done February 5, 1788."

Billet, or Tip-cat, was also a popular game for this day, and in some parts of the North of England it is customary for the girls to occupy some part of the festival by the game of battledoor and shuttlecock, singing : —

SHROVE-TIDE, OR CARNIVAL.

> "Great A, little A,
> This is Pancake Day;
> Toss the ball high,
> Throw the ball low,
> Those that come after
> May sing heigh-ho!"

In Sir John Sinclair's "Statistical Account of Scotland," 1795, we read: "On Shrove-Tuesday there is a standing match at foot-ball between the married and unmarried women, in which the former are always victorious." In the same work we read: "Every year on Shrove-Tuesday the bachelors and married men drew themselves up at the Cross of Scone on opposite sides. A ball was then thrown up, and they played from two o'clock till sunset."

This custom is supposed to have had its origin in the days of chivalry. An Italian, it is said, came into this part of the country, challenging all the parishes under a certain penalty in case of declining his challenge. All the parishes declined the challenge except Scone, which beat the foreigner, and in commemoration of this gallant action the game was instituted. Whilst the custom continued, every man in the parish, the gentry not excepted, was obliged to turn out and support the side to which he belonged, and the person who neglected to do his part on that occasion was fined.

A singular old custom or strife in Kent, different from the above, is thus described in the "Gentleman's

Magazine," 1772. The custom appears to be a remnant of ancient Carnival or Shrove-tide merriment, of which but few traces are now to be found among the popular observances of the times : —

> "Being on a visit on Tuesday last, in a little obscure village in this county, I found an odd kind of sport going forward; the girls, from eighteen to five or six years old, were assembled in a crowd, and burning an uncouth effigy, which they called an Holly-boy, and which it seems they had stolen from the boys; who, in another part of the village, were assembled together and burning what they called an Ivy-girl, which they had stolen from the girls. All this ceremony was accompanied with loud huzzas, noise, and acclamations. What it all means I cannot tell, although I inquired of several of the oldest people in the place, who could only answer that it had always been a sport at this season of the year."

The holly and the ivy being Christmas evergreens, the ceremony described may perhaps have been a facetious way of signifying that the Christmas holidays were at last come to an end.

The following quaint old carol of the time of Henry VI. seems to have reference to some such custom as that just described : —

NAY, IVY, NAY!

> "Nay, Ivy, nay, it shall not be, I wis,
>   Let Holly have the mastery, as the manner is.
>   Holly standeth in the hall fair to behold,
>   Ivy stands without the door; she is full sore a cold.
>   Nay, Ivy, nay, etc.

SHROVE-TIDE, OR CARNIVAL.

"Holly and his merry men, they dance now and they sing;
Ivy and her maidens, they weep, and their hands wring.
                    Nay, Ivy, nay, etc.

"Ivy hath a lybe,[1] she caught it with the cold,
So may they all have, that do with Ivy hold.
                    Nay, Ivy, nay, etc.

"Holly he hath berries, as red as any rose,
The foresters, the hunters, keep them from the does.
                    Nay, Ivy, nay, etc.

"Ivy she hath berries, as black as any sloe,
There come the owls and eat them as they go.
                    Nay, Ivy, nay, etc.

"Holly he hath birds, a full fair flock,
The nightingale, the poppinjay, the gentle laverock.
                    Nay, Ivy, nay, etc.

"Good Ivy say to us, what birds hast thou?
None but the owlet that cries, 'How! How!'
                    Nay, Ivy, nay," etc.

The following from Mr. Wright's MS. seems also to have reference to this sylvan warfare, which appears to have been conducted with rustic courtesy, and in the true spirit of chivalry:—

"Holly and Ivy made a great party,
Who should have the mastery
    In lands where they go.

---

[1] The word is not explained by any glossary.

"Then spake Holly, 'I am fierce and jolly,
I will have the mastery
In lands where we go.'

"Then spake Ivy, 'I am loud and proud,
And I will have the mastery
In lands where we go.'

"Then spake Holly, and bent him down on his knee,
'I pray thee, gentle Ivy, essay me no villainy,
In lands where we go.'"

NOTE.—Fosbrooke says: "The sports on Shrove-Tuesday being vestiges of the Romish carnivals, masquerades and processions were made, and effigies called Holly-boys and Ivy-girls were burned."

CHAPTER X.

EASTER.

THE term Easter is derived, as some suppose, from the Saxon "Oster," to rise; this being the day of Christ's rising from the dead. Others, however, maintain that this Queen of Christian festivals, takes its name from Eoster, or Easter, a Saxon goddess whose religious rites were celebrated in the beginning of Spring.

Soane suggests that the Saxon *Easter* or *Eoster*, the Greek 'Αστήρ, the

English *Star*, and the Hebrew *Ashtaroth*, have all come from the same long-forgotten original, perhaps Phœnician, word signifying " Fire."

It was anciently the custom in England to put out all the fires and relight them on Easter-Even, from consecrated flints preserved in churches specially for that purpose. The popular belief was that holy fire, obtained in this manner, would prevent the effect of storms, etc. Fosbrooke, quoting Rupert, says, " The flint signified Christ, and the fire the Holy Ghost."

The custom of putting out the fire in the hall also at this season, appears to have been connected with this ecclesiastical observance. The "Festival" (1511), referring to this domestic usage, says : —

" This day (Easter) is called, in many places, Goddes Sondaye ; ye know well that it is the maner at this daye to do the fyre out of the hall, and the black Wynter brandes, and all thynges that is foule with fume and smoke shall be done awaye, and there the fyre was, shall be gayly arayed with fayre flowres, and strewed with grene rysshes all aboute."

Dr. Drake in his work, " Shakespeare and his Times," says that, " Easter was formerly a season of great social festivities ; " and also that, " it was customary for the common people — even as they do still in Ireland — to rise early on Easter morning to see the sun dance." Metaphorically considered, that thought may be termed both just and beautiful ; for as " the earth and her valleys standing thick with corn " are said to "laugh and sing," so, on account of the glory of the Resurrection, the sun may be said to "dance" for joy — the natural rising of the sun being, as it were, typical of the rising of the Sun of Righteousness from the darkness of the grave. The earth also, awaking at this season from its death-like wintry slumber, seems to make an appropriate response to this celestial demonstration of joy by its own most beautiful Easter offering of Spring flowers.

This idea has been happily expressed by Paulinus, Bishop of Nola (431): —

"Sing praises to your God, ye youths, and pay your holy vows,
The floor with many flowers strew, the threshold bind with
  boughs;
Let Winter breathe a fragrance forth, like as the purple Spring;
Let the young year, before the time, its floral treasures bring,
And Nature yield, to this Great Day, herself an offering."

The use of these flowers at the Easter festival has of late gradually become more and more popular. Our forefathers, in addition to this pious use of flowers, had besides, even in their holiday recreations, an allusion to this fundamental doctrine of Christianity.

Some of the sports and pastimes referred to appear to us childish and absurd, but in other times, before the world had become so very wise as at present, they may have been, to simple-minded people, very edifying. One of the most curious of these popular observances is that of "lifting" or "heaving," as it was called, a custom which still lingers in some counties in England. The ceremony has been thus described : —

"On Easter-Monday the men lift the women; and on Easter-Tuesday the women lift, or heave, the men. The process is performed by two lusty men, or women, joining their hands across each other's wrists; then, making the person to be heaved, sit down on their arms, they lift him up aloft three times, and often carry him several yards along a street. At the end of the ceremony the person lifted is duly kissed by the lifters, and a forfeit claimed. Sometimes, instead of crossed hands, a chair or bed is used."

The custom is supposed to be a vulgar representation of the Resurrection. Perhaps also the Lesson for Easter Even might have suggested this singular species of merriment, for there we find that, "Corn shall make the young men *cheerful,* and *new wine* the maids." Indeed the Church services seem often to have suggested to the people similar jocular ideas. Mr. Ellis inserts in his edition of Brand's "Popular Antiquities," a letter from Mr. Thomas Loggan, of Basinghall Street, London, in which he says : —

"I was sitting alone last Easter-Tuesday at breakfast, at the Talbot Inn, Shrewsbury, when I was surprised by the entrance of all the female servants of the house handing in an arm-chair, lined with white, and decorated with ribbons and favors of different colors. I asked them what they wanted : their answer was, they came to heave me; it was the custom of the place on that morning, and they hoped I would take a seat in their chair. It was impossible not to comply with a request very modestly made, and by a set of nymphs in their best apparel, and several of them under twenty. I wished to see all the ceremony, and seated myself accordingly. The group then lifted me from the ground, turned the chair about, and I had the felicity of a salute from each. I told them I supposed there was a fee on the occasion, and was answered in the affirmative, and having satisfied the damsels in this respect, they withdrew to heave others. At this time I had never heard of such a custom; but on inquiry I found that on Easter-Monday, between nine and twelve, the men heave the women, in the same manner as on the Tuesday, between the same hours, the women heave the men."

This custom, it appears, is of undoubted antiquity, for we find from a roll in the custody of the Keeper of the Records in the Tower of London, that certain ladies and maids of honor received payment for taking King Edward I. in his bed at Easter: —

"To the ladies of the Queen's chamber 15th of May; seven ladies and damsels of the Queen, because they took (or lifted) the King in his bed, on the morrow of Easter, and made him pay fine for the peace of the King, which he made of his gift by the hand of Hugh de Cerr (or Kerr), Esq., to the Lady of Weston, £14."

Perhaps the nursery pastime of "making a chair," still in vogue among children, is a relic of this ancient custom.

The game of hand-ball, however, another of the Easter sports, appears to have had a very different fortune, and to have developed itself into those most manly of athletic sports, the modern base-ball and cricket.

In ancient times, say the Ritualists Belethus and Durandus —

" The bishops and archbishops on the Continent used to recreate themselves in the game of hand-ball with their inferior clergy ; and in England, also, the game appears to have been made a part of the regular Church service at Chester. Bishops and deans took the ball into the Cathedral, and at the commencement of the antiphon, began to dance, throwing the ball to the choristers, who handed it to each other during the time of the dancing and antiphon."[1]

Nor was it uncommon in England for corporate bodies to amuse themselves at this game, with their burgesses and young people. Such was once the custom, says Mr. Brand, at Newcastle, at the Feasts of Easter and Whitsuntide, when the mayor, aldermen, and sheriff, accompanied by great numbers of the burgesses, used to go yearly at these seasons to the Forth or little mall of the town, with mace, sword, and cap of maintenance carried before them, and not only countenance, but frequently join in, the diversions of hand-ball, dancing, etc. There was also in the ancient city of Chester a similar custom, when at the great Festival of Easter, " The mayor and corporation, with the twenty guilds established in Chester, with their wardens at their heads, set forth in all their pageantry to the Rood-eye (an open meadow by the river side); to

---

[1] Dancing was at first, and indeed during some thousands of years, a religious ceremony. In the Temples of Jerusalem, Samaria, and Alexandria, a stage for these exercises was erected in one part, thence called the choir, the name of which has been preserved in our churches, and the custom too, it seems, till within a few centuries. The Cardinal Ximenes revived in his time the practice of Mosarabic Masses in the Cathedral of Toledo, when the people danced, both in the choir and in the nave, with great decorum and devotion.

play at foot-ball. The mayor with his mace, sword, and cap of maintenance, stood before the Cross, whilst the guild of shoemakers, to whom the right had belonged from time immemorial, presented him with the ball of the value of ' three and four-pence or above,' and all set to work right merrily." But as too often falls out in this game, "great strife did arise among the younge persons of the same cittie," and hence, in the time of Henry VIII., this piece of homage to the mayor was converted into a present from the shoemakers to the drapers, of six gleaves or hand-darts of silver, to be given for the best foot-race; whilst the saddlers, who went in procession on horseback, attired in all their bravery, each carrying a spear with a wooden ball, decorated with flowers and arms, exchanged their offering for a silver bell, which should be a "reward for that horse which with speedy runninge should run before all others." These silver bells were in the seventeenth century converted into cups, or other pieces of plate, which still continue to be the "trophies of victory" at horse-races.

But the ordinary prize at games of ball during Easter, was the Tansy-cake: —

> "At stool-ball, Lucia, let us play
> For sugar cakes and wine;
> Or for a tansy let us play,
> The loss be thine or mine.

> "If thou, my dear, a winner be,
>   At trundling of the ball,
> The wager thou shalt have and me,
>   And my misfortunes all."

These cakes were made of flour, butter, sugar, sherry, cream, and tansies; whence they derived the name of "tansays," or "tansy-cakes." The tansy having reference, says Selden, to the *bitter herbs* used by the Jews at the Passover, though at the same time, " 'twas always the fashion, for a man to have a gammon of bacon to show himself to be no Jew." The Jews themselves, however, says Brady, in his "Clavis Calendaria," "long since contrived to diminish the bitter flavor of the tansy, by making it into a pickle for their Paschal Lamb, from whence we borrowed the custom of taking mint and sugar as a general sauce for that description of food."

Another custom which prevailed in the olden time, and which is still kept up both in England and Ireland, and even in this country, is that of presenting children with eggs, stained with various colors in boiling, and curiously ornamented with devices and mottoes; they are termed "paste," or more properly "Pasche Eggs." In the Greek Church likewise, says Brady, "*Eggs* still continue to form a part of the ceremonies of the day; and *there* also, presents of eggs, from one individual to another, are considered as pious attentions." This observance appears to have arisen from a belief that eggs were an emblem of the Resurrection. On this custom Mr. Brand has well observed that —

" The ancient Egyptians, if the resurrection of the body had been a tenet of their faith, would perhaps have thought an egg no improper hieroglyphical representation of it. The exclusion of a living creature by incubation, after the vital principle has lain so long dormant or extinct, is a process so truly marvelous, that if it could be disbelieved, would be thought by some a thing as incredible, as that the Author of Life should be able to reanimate the dead."

In the "Ritual" of Pope Paul V., which was composed for the use of the British Isles, there is this prayer for the consecration of eggs : —

" Bless, O Lord, we beseech thee, this thy creature of eggs, that it may become a wholesome sustenance to thy faithful servants, eating it in thankfulness to thee, on account of the Resurrection of our Lord."

In Lancashire and Cheshire, children still go round the village and beg eggs for the Easter dinner, accompanying their solicitation by a short song, the burden of which is addressed to the farmer's dame, asking for "an egg, bacon, cheese, or an apple, or any good thing that will make us merry ; " and ending with, " And I pray you good dame an Easter egg."

The observance in Lancashire of " Pace-egging," as it is there called, is a custom limited to the week preceding Easter Day, commencing on the Monday and finishing on the Thursday before Easter Day.

"Young men in groups, varying in number from three to twenty, dressed in various fantastic garbs, and wearing masks, some of the groups accompanied by a player or two on the violin, go from house to house singing, dancing, and capering. At most places they are liberally treated with wine, punch, or ale, dealt out to them by the host or hostess."

The origin of this custom of collecting "Pasche eggs," may have been the resumption on the part of our forefathers of eggs and of animal food at Easter, on the termination of Lent. It seems, moreover, that at this season extreme caution was to be used in partaking of food of all kinds, and nothing was to be eaten which had not been previously blessed, or had not at least the sign of the Cross made over it; for the faithful were thought just then to be particularly subject to the attacks of evil spirits. Durandus gives a lamentable instance of the fatal consequences arising from a neglect of this precaution, and of which he was himself an eye-witness: "Two devils got possession of a young girl, and tormented her for three years," a miracle which, says Mr. Soane, "is often renewed in our own days, but with this especial difference, that when the devil now possesses a woman, he does not torment herself but others." "However, on this occasion, a cunning exorcist drove the fiends out at last, having previously made them confess that they had been lying perdu in a melon, which the girl had incautiously eaten without first making the sign of the Cross."

There has been a revival in modern times, even in this country, of the old Easter custom of "pace-egging." We refer to the usage of presenting one's friends on the morning of Easter Day, with a basket of pace-eggs. A dozen of these, of various colors, with mottoes and emblematic devices, artistically arranged in a fancy basket, make indeed a very appropriate Easter decoration for the drawing-room table, seeming to greet us with that most ancient of Easter salutations (still retained in the Greek Church), "Christ is risen!"

CHAPTER XI.

ROGATION WEEK.

AN inquiry into the social festivities of the Easter Holidays naturally brings us to the consideration of those parochial perambulations which in England, formerly, and even now in many places, distinguish the celebration of the Rogation Week. Perhaps some account of these ceremonial observances may be of interest to us, especially to those engaged in rural proceedings of a character somewhat similar.

These rural perambulations do not with us by any means necessarily take place in Rogation Week, nor are there now in force here any royal or episcopal injunctions similar to those issued in the days of Queen Elizabeth, when by —

"Advertisements partly for due order in the public administration of Common Prayers, &c., by virtue of the Queene's Majesties' Letters commanding the same, it was directed, 'item, that, in the Rogation[1] Daies of procession, they singe or saye in Englishe, the two Psalmes beginnyng "*Benedic anima mea,*" *&c., with the Letanye & suffrages thereunto, with one homelye of thankesgevying to God,*' already devised and divided into foure partes, without addition of any superstitious ceremoneys heretofore used.' "

But still the devout motive for such ritual observances as those formerly enjoined, should be as potent now as in the days of Elizabeth.

Our Sunday and parochial schools have, however, already established an annual picnic, with rural processionings having more or less of ritual solemnity. They have their banners and their psalm-singing, and they might have also their "*Gospel Trees,*" of which poets have sung, for there are noble elms enough in the country to serve that purpose, and there are fountains whose pure sparkling waters are as deserving of floral crowns as those picturesque wells at Tissington, in Derbyshire (hereafter mentioned).

The ancient custom of Perambulating or "Beating

---

[1] Also called "Gange Daies," derived from the Saxon word "gangen," *to go.*

the Bounds" of parishes, in Rogation Week, had, it is said, a twofold object. It was designed to supplicate the divine blessing on the fruits of the earth, and to preserve in all classes of the community a correct knowledge of, and due respect for, the bounds of parochial and individual property.

> "That every man might keep his own possessions,
> Our fathers used in reverent processions,
> (With zealous prayers, and with praisefull cheere),
> To walk the parish limits once a year."—
>
> *Wither,* 1635.

It appears that these Rogation ceremonies originated in the fifth century. In an age, says Dean Stanley, —

"Gloomy with disaster and superstition, when heathenism was still struggling with Christianity; when Christianity was disfigured by fierce conflicts within the Church; when the Roman Empire was tottering to its ruin; when the last great luminary of the Church — Augustine — had just passed away, amidst the forebodings of universal destruction. The general disorder of the time was aggravated by an unusual train of calamities. Besides the ruin of society attendant on the invasion of the barbarians, there came a succession of droughts, pestilences, and earthquakes, which seemed to keep pace with the throes of the moral world. Of all these horrors, France was the centre. On one of these occasions, when the people had been hoping that with the Easter festival, some respite would come, a sudden earthquake shook the church at Vienne, on the Rhone. It was on Easter Eve; the congregation rushed out; the Bishop of the city (Mamertus) was left alone before the altar. On that terrible night he formed a resolution of inventing a new form, as he hoped, of drawing down the mercy of God. He determined that in the three days before Ascension Day, there should be a long procession to the nearest churches in the neighborhood. For four hundred years there were no prayers of this special kind in the Christian Church. The traveller who passes that beautiful old city (Vienne), on his way through France, may treasure up as he hurries by, the thought that along the banks of that rushing river, and from height to height of those encircling hills, were first heard the sounds of the Litany which are now so familiar. It was under a like pressure of calamities that the Litany first became part of our services."

It is the earliest portion of the " Book of Common Prayer" in its present English form.

It is not easy to say when or how these " Rogations" became mixed up with the parochial perambulations, but there cannot be the least doubt that the latter have been derived to us from the times of the Romans. It is said to be only a Christian form of the *Terminalia*, established by Numa Pompilius in honor of the God Terminus, the guardian of fields and landmarks, and maintainer of peace amongst mankind.

Before the Reformation, parochial perambulations were conducted with great state and ceremony. The lord of the manor, with a large banner, priests in surplices and with crosses, and other persons with handbells and staves, followed by most of the parishioners, walked in procession round the parish, stopping at crosses, forming crosses on the ground, saying or singing gospels to the corn, and allowing drinkings and good cheer.

Boundaries of parishes and townships were, in many points, marked out by what are called "Gospel-trees." Herrick, that stanch maintainer of old English customs, in "Hesperides," says:—

> "Dearest, bury me
> Under that Holy Oak, or Gospel Tree;
> Where, though thou see'st not, thou may'st
> Think upon me, when thou *yearly go'st procession.*"

In Kentish Town, London, there still stands a public-house, which bears the significant sign of the Gospel Oak, taking its name from an old oak in the neighborhood, a relic of the olden time, suggestive of the once general custom of reading a portion of the Gospel for the day under certain trees, in the parish perambulations.

"In 1554," says Strype, "the priests of Queen Mary's chapel, made public processions. All the three days there went her chapel about the fields: the first to St. Giles', and there sung Mass: the next day, being Tuesday, to St. Martin's-in-the-Fields; and there a sermon was preached, and Mass sung; and the company drank there: the third day to Westminster, where a sermon was made, and then Mass and good cheer made; and after about the park, and so to St. James's Court.

"The same Rogation Week, went out of the Tower on procession priests and clerks, and the Lieutenant, with all his waiters and the axe of the Tower borne in procession; the waits[1] attended. There

---

[1] The waits here mentioned were minstrels. At this time, it appears there were few towns of any size or note in England that did not support a band of waits, who wore a peculiar costume. Those of the city of London appeared on state occasions, in blue gowns with red sleeves, with silver badges suspended from silver collars.

joined in this procession the inhabitants also of St. Catharine's, Radcliff, Limehouse, Poplar, Stratford, Bow, Shoreditch, and all those that belonged to the Tower, with their Halberts. They went about the fields of St. Catherine's and the Liberties.

"On the following Thursday, being Holy Thursday, or Ascension-Day, at the Court of St. James's, with heralds and sergeants of arms, and four Bishops, mitred, and Bishop Bonner, besides his mitre, wore a pair of slippers of silver and gold, and a pair of rich gloves with ouches of silver upon them, very rich."

At the Reformation, says the "Book of Days," the ceremonies and practices deemed objectionable, were considerably modified, and a homily was prepared for the occasion, and injunctions were issued by royal authority, requiring that for "the perambulations of the circuits of the parishes, the people should, once a year, at the time accustomed, with the rector, vicar, or curate, walk about the parishes as they were accustomed, and at their return to the church make their common prayer. And the curate, in their said common perambulations, was at certain convenient places to admonish the people to give thanks to God (while beholding of his benefits) and for the increase and abundance of his fruits upon the face of the Earth, with the singing of the 103d Psalm."

In strict accordance with these directions, we find that "the judicious Hooker" — a faithful exemplar of a true English churchman — duly observed the custom of perambulations. At such times, he would, says his biographer, "honest Isaac Walton," "usually express more pleasant discourse than at other times, and would then always drop some loving and facetious observations to be remembered against the next year, especially by the boys and young people, still inclining them, and all his present parishioners, to meekness and mutual kindness and love; *because love thinks not evil, but covers a multitude of infirmities."*

It seems, however, that sometimes instead of loving and facetious observations, sound floggings were administered to the boys, for the same desirable purpose of strengthening their memory.

The "Saturday Review" (February 15, 1868), on this subject says:—

"At the yearly ceremony of beating parish boundaries, it was usual to beat not only the boundaries, but the boys; or rather, perhaps, the phrase of 'beating' has been inaccurately transferred from the boys to the boundaries."[1]

In Herbert's "Country Parson," also, we are told:—

"The Country Parson is a lover of old customs, if they be good and harmlesse. Particularly he loves *Procession*, and maintains it, because there are contained therein four manifest advantages. First, a blessing of God for the fruits of the field. 2. Justice in the

---

[1] There is a curious old Norman record illustrative of this "beating" principle: "Duke Robert, just on the point of going to the Holy Land, made a gift to the Abbey of Preaux. His son, the future Conqueror, '*adhuc puerulus*,' was sent to lay the deed of gift on the altar. Let no one suppose that irreverent hands were laid on the person of the great Bastard, even at the age of seven years. But then and there, in the young prince's presence, three other boys had their ears solemnly boxed that they might remember all about it, "*ob causam memoriæ colaphum susceperant.*"

preservation of bounds. 3. Charitie in loving, walking, and neighbourly accompanying one another, with reconciling of differences at that time, if there be any. 4. Mercie, in relieving the poor by a liberal distribution and largess, which at that time is or ought to be used. Wherefore he exacts of all to be present at the Perambulation, and those that withdraw and sever themselves from it he mislikes, and reproves as uncharitable and unneighbourly ; and if they will not reforme, presents them."

It appears that the ecclesiastic authorities at this time insisted particularly upon the religious observances of these parochial perambulations. In the Articles of Enquiry for the Archdeaconry of Northumberland, the following occurs : " Doth your Parson or Vicar observe the Three Rogation Dayes?" In others, for the Diocese of Chichester, 1637, is the subsequent question : —

"Doth your minister yeerely, in Rogation Weeke, for the knowing and distinguishing of the bounds of parishes, and for obtaining God's blessing upon the fruites of the ground, walke the Perambulation, and say, or sing, in English, the Gospells, Epistles, Letanie, and other devout prayers ; together with the 103rd and 104th Psalmes?"

The necessity or determination to perambulate precisely along the old track, often occasioned curious incidents. If a canal had been cut through the boundary of a parish, it was deemed necessary that some of the parishioners should pass through the water. Where a river formed part of the boundary line, the procession either passed along it in boats, or some of the party stripped and swam along it, or boys were thrown into it at customary places. If a house had been erected on the boundary line, the procession claimed the right to pass through it. A ludicrous scene, it is said, occurred in London about the beginning of the present century. As the procession of church-wardens, parish officers, etc., followed by a concourse of cads, were perambulating the parish of St. George's, Hanover Square, they came to the part of a street where a nobleman's coach was standing just across the boundary line. The carriage was empty, waiting for the owner, who was in the opposite house; the principal church-warden, — himself a nobleman, — therefore desired the coachman to drive out of their way. "I won't," said the sturdy coachman, "my lord told me to wait here, and here I will wait till his lordship tells me to move!" The church-warden coolly opened the carriage door, entered it, passed out through the opposite door, and was followed by the whole procession, cads, sweeps, and scavengers.

The religious part of these processions has, according to Mr. Chambers, been generally omitted in more modern times.

"The custom has, however, of late years been revived in its integrity in many parishes; and certainly, such perambulations among the bounties of creation, afford a Christian minister a most favorable opportunity for awakening in his parishioners a due sense of gratitude towards him who maketh the sun to shine, and the rains to descend upon the earth, so that it may bring forth its fruit in due season."

ROGATION WEEK.

These perambulations occasionally took place on Ascension Day, — celebrated springs or fountains, instead of *Gospel-trees*, sometimes serving as stations. Aubrey says: —

"In Cheshire when they went in perambulation, they did blesse the springs, i. e. they did read a Gospell at them, and did believe the water was the better."[1]

An interesting account of such a ceremony as this in what is called "The Dressing of the Wells of Tissington," is given by a correspondent of "Chambers' Book of Days" (page 596). This custom seems, from the parish record, to have originated in 1615, a year of remarkable drought, when these wells furnished to the inhabitants and their cattle for ten miles round an unfailing supply of water, an element of which the English, in their moist climate, have seldom experienced the want.

"When we drove into the village, though it was only ten o'clock, we found it already full of people from many miles round, who had assembled to celebrate the feast; for such indeed it was, all the characteristics of a village wake being there in the shape of booths, nuts, gingerbread, and toys, to delight the young. We went immediately to the church, foreseeing the difficulty there would be in getting a seat, nor were we mistaken, for though we were accommodated, numbers were obliged to remain outside, and wait for the service peculiar to the wells. The interior of the church is orna-

[1] We read that once in the wilderness, in a time of drought at Beer the promised well, Israel sang this song, "Spring up, O well; sing ye unto it." — *Num.* xxi. 17.

mented with many monuments of the Fitzherbert family, and the service was performed in rural style by a band of violinists who did their best to make melody. As soon as the sermon was ended, the clergyman left the pulpit, and marched at the head of the procession that was formed, into the village. After him came the band; then the family from the Hall, and then visitors, the rest of the congregation following; and a halt was made at the first of the wells, which are five in number, and which we will now attempt to describe.

"The name of 'well' scarcely gives a proper idea of these beautiful structures; they are rather fountains, or cascades, the water descending from above, and not rising, as in a well. Their height varies from ten to twelve feet; and the original stone frontage is on this day hidden by a wooden erection in the form of an arch, or some other elegant design; over these planks a layer of plaster of Paris is spread, and while it is wet, flowers without leaves are stuck in it, forming a most beautiful mosaic pattern On one the large yellow field Ranunculus was arranged in letters, and so a verse of Scripture, or of a hymn, was recalled to the spectator's mind; on another, a white dove was sculptured in the plaster, and set in a groundwork of the humble violet; the daisy, which our poet Chaucer would gaze upon for hours together, formed a diaper work of red and white; the pale yellow primrose was set off by the rich red of the ribes; nor were the coral berries of the holly, mountain-ash, and yew, forgotten; these are carefully gathered and stored in the winter to be ready for the May-day fête. It is scarcely possible to describe the vivid coloring and beautiful effect of these favorites of nature, arranged in wreaths and garlands and devices of every hue. And then, the pure, sparkling water, which pours down from the midst of them unto the rustic moss-grown stones beneath, completes the enchantment, and makes this feast of the 'well-flowering' one of the most beautiful of all the old customs that are left in 'Merrie England.'

"The groups of visitors and country people, dressed in their holiday clothes, stood reverently round, whilst the clergyman read the first of the three psalms appointed for the day, and then gave out one of Bishop Heber's beautiful hymns, in which all joined with heart and voice.

"When this was all over, all moved forwards to the next well, where the next psalm was read, and another hymn sung; the Epistle and Gospel being read at the last two wells. The service was now over, and the people dispersed to wander through the village or park, which is thrown open; the cottagers vie with each other in showing hospitality to the strangers, and many kettles are boiled at their fires, for those who have brought the materials for a picnic on the green. It is welcomed as a season of mirth and good fellowship, many old friends meeting there to separate for another year, should they be spared to see the Well-dressing again, whilst the young people enjoy their games and country pastimes with their usual vivacity."

The foregoing account might perhaps furnish us with a model, or hints, for similar excursions in the country.

" Still, Dovedale, yield thy flowers to deck the fountains
　　Of Tissington upon its holiday ;
The customs long preserved among the mountains
　　Should not be lightly left to pass away;
They have their moral ; and we often may
　　Learn from them how our wise forefathers wrought,
When they upon the public mind would lay
　　Some weighty principle, some maxim brought
Home to their hearts, the healthful product of deep thought." —
　　　　　　　　　　　　　　Edwards.

CHAPTER XII.

WHITSUNTIDE.

THERE is some dispute among the learned as to the meaning of the word Whitsun; it is said by some to have been derived from the custom in the Primitive Church of the catechumens wearing white garments, or chrisoms, at this time, which was then observed as one of the two principal seasons of public baptism. Dr. Neale, however, thinks it curious "that the name *Whitsun-*

day should be thus mistaken. It is neither *White Sunday* (for in truth the color is red), nor *Huit* Sunday, as the *eighth* after Easter; but simply by the various corruptions of the German *Pfingsten*, the Dansk *Pinste*, the various patois *Pingsten*, *Whingsten*, etc., derived from Pentecost." In proof of the above, note that it is not Easter *Sunday*, but Easter *Day*, so it is not Whit *Sunday* but *Whitsun Day;* and we speak of Whitsun Week, just as they do of Pfingsten Woche, in German. Whatever may have been the origin of the term, Whitsuntide has been from the earliest times observed in England, as in Germany, by the celebration of all sorts of outdoor sports and pastimes. It was at this season, also, that the Whitsun Ales were held — those "drinking assemblies" at which parishioners were expected to drink ale for the especial good of their souls; when the church-wardens sold the ale to the populace, in the church-yard, and to the better sort, as it is said, even in the church itself, the profits being set apart (as in our modern fairs) for the repair or decoration of the church, and for the maintenance of the poor. On these occasions were witnessed those exhibitions of archery which once made Old England famous throughout all the world; and also matches at running and wrestling, with other athletic sports. England, as Shakespeare says, was then —

"Busied with a Whitsun morris-dance."

The mummers also appear again with —

"Robin Hood and his merry men all,"

and St. George — who at Christmas was but a carpet-knight — now literally "takes the field," or rather *to* the field. Nor was music wanting on these occasions to enliven the sports; for besides the bells of the morris-dancers, there were the pipe and tabor in modern times, and the harp and viol in the days of more remote antiquity, according to an old ballad : —

"Harke, harke, I heare the dancing,
And a nimble morris-prancing;
The bagpipe and the morris-bells,
That they are not far hence us tells;
Come let us all goe thither,
And dance like friends together."

It is to us in America an interesting fact, connected with these Whitsuntide observances, that the voyager Sir Humphrey Gilbert, in an expedition fitted out by him under royal commission, sailing from Dartmouth in *June* 1583, and which planted the first *English* colony west of the Atlantic, "provided," says Mr. Hayes, the historian of the voyage, "for the solace of our own people, and the allurement of the savages, music in good variety, not omitting the least toys, as morris-dancers, hobby-horses, and May-like conceits to delight the savage people."

But before proceeding with an account of these

Whitsun Ales, we propose to notice briefly a singular piece of ecclesiastical pageantry formerly connected in popular estimation with the joyous celebration of Whitsuntide.

Before the invention of printing, such religious shows were to the people very much what books and pictures are to us. The machinery then used seems ludicrous to us with our superior advantages, but it by no means follows that it appeared so to them.

But to illustrate: Whitsuntide then, it appears, was anciently distinguished from all other holidays by a singular display of fire-works of a peculiar ecclesiastical character, calculated, as was supposed, to represent to the people the descent of the Holy Ghost on the Day of Pentecost. The "Bee-hive of the Romish Church," speaking of these satirically, says:—

"They send downe a dove out of an owle's nest devised in the roof of the church; but first they cast out rosin and gunpowder, with wild-fire, to make the children afraid, and that must needs be the Holie Ghost which cometh with thunder and lightning."

But perhaps Mr. Fosbrooke's account of this extraordinary spectacle will best exemplify the custom referred to:—

"This feast," says he, "was celebrated in Spain with representations of the gift of the Holy Ghost, and of thunder from engines, which did much damage. Wafers or cakes, preceded by water, oak-leaves, or burning torches, were thrown down from the church roof; small birds with cakes tied to their legs, and pigeons were let loose;

sometimes there were tame white ones tied with strings, or one of wood suspended. A long censer was also swung up and down."

From the same learned author we find also the following : —

"In an old computus, Anno 1509, of St. Patrick's, Dublin, we have iv^s vii^d paid to those playing with the great and little angel and the dragon ; iii^s paid for little cords employed about the Holy Ghost ; iv^s vi^d for making the angel (thurifurcantis) censing, and ii^s ii^d for cords of it — all on the Feast of Pentecost."

But in the British Isles, with the dawn of the Reformation, all remnants of these extraordinary and exceptional pyrotechnic exhibitions disappeared, and there remain now only for consideration those customs and usages the relics of which have survived, and which more properly belong to the Whitsuntide of our English forefathers.

Easter Ales and Whitsun Ales, so called from their being held on Easter Sunday and on Whitsunday, or on some of the holidays that follow them, originated from the wakes. These wakes, according to Mr. Strutt, were primitively held upon the day of the dedication of the church, or on the birthday of the saint whose relics were therein deposited, or to whose honor it was consecrated. The generosity of the founder and endower thereof was at the same time celebrated, and a service composed suitable to the occasion. This is still done in the Colleges of Oxford, to the memory of the respective founders. On the eve of this day, prayers were said and hymns were sung all night in the church; and from these watchings the festivals were styled "wakes;" which name still continues in many parts of England, although the vigils have been long in disuse.

These wakes when first established, it is said, greatly resembled the Agapœ, or Love-Feasts, of the early Christians. In process of time, however, the people assembled on the vigil, or evening preceding the saint's day, and came, says a quaint old author, "to churche with candellys burnyng, and would wake, and come towards night to the churche in their devocion."

The old author above quoted on the subject of these wakes, mentions certain scandalous excesses into which the people had gradually fallen, unmindful of an ancient canon which required that, "Those who came to the wake should pray devoutly and not betake themselves to drunkenness and debauchery,"—vices to which it seems our Anglo-Saxon forefathers were always too much inclined; he says: "And afterwards the people fell to letcherie and songs, and daunces, with harping and piping, and also to glotony and sinne; and so tourned the holyness to cursydness."

Whatsoever truth there may have been in these serious charges, it is certain that in proportion as these festivals deviated from the original design of their institution, they increased in popularity, the conviviality was extended, and not only the inhabitants of the parish to which the church belonged were present at them, but they were joined by others from the neighboring towns and parishes.

The church-wardens and other chief officers of the church, observing these wakes to be more popular than any other holidays, shrewdly conceived that by establishing other institutions somewhat similar to them, they might draw together a large company of people, and annually collect from them, gratuitously as it were, such sums of money for the support and repairs of the church, as would be a great easement to the parish rates. By way of enticement to the populace, they brewed a certain portion of strong ale, to be ready on the day appointed for the festival, which they sold to them; and most of the better sort, in addition to what they paid for their drink, contributed something towards the collection; but in some instances, the inhabitants of one or more parishes were mulcted in a certain sum, according to mutual agreement, as appears by an ancient stipulation couched in the following terms: —

"The parishioners of Elvertoon and those of Okebrook in Derbyshire, agree jointly to brew four ales, and every ale of one quarter of malt, between this and the Feast of St. John the Baptist next coming, and every inhabitant of the said town of Okebrook shall be at the several Ales; and every husband and his wife shall pay two pence; and every cottager one penny. And the inhabitants of Elvertoon shall have and receive all the profits coming of the said ales, to the use and behoof of the church of Elvertoon; and the inhabitants of Elvertoon shall brew eight ales betwixt this and the Feast of St. John, at which ales the inhabitants of Okebrook shall come and pay as before rehearsed; and if any be away one ale, he is to pay at t'oder ale for both."

Stubbs, on the subject of these ales, says: —

"In certain townes where drunken Bacchus bears sway, against Christmass and Easter, Whitsunday, or some other time, the church-wardens — for so they call them — of every parish, with the consent of the whole parish, provide half a score or twentie quarters of mault, whereof some they buy of the church stocke, and some is given to them of the parishioners themselves, every one conferring somewhat, according to his ability; which mault being made into very strong ale, or beer, is set to sale, either in the church, or in some other place assigned to that. Then, when this nippitatum, this huffe-cappe, as they call it, this nectar of life, is set abroach, well is he that can get the soonest to it, and spends the most at it, for he is counted the godliest man of all the rest, and most in God's favour, because it is spent upon his church forsooth! If all be true which they say, they bestow that money which is got thereby, for the repair of their churches and chappels; they buy books for the service, cupps for the celebration of the Sacrament, surplesses for Sir John (the parson), and such other necessaries, &c."

In reading the above, some allowance should be made for the prejudices of Stubbs, who was one of those puritanical zealots whose reformatory labors in the succeeding century so disastrously ended in a general subversion of all things both in Church and State.

However, those more charitably disposed will much prefer the benevolent good humor of honest Old

Aubrey, that eminent antiquary of the seventeenth century, whose character for veracity, it is said, has never been impeached: —

"There were no rates for the poor in my grandfather's days, says he, but for Kingston St. Michael (no small parish) the church ale at Whitsuntide did the business. In every parish is, or was, a church-house, to which belonged spits, crocks, etc., utensils for dressing provisions. Here the housekeepers met and were merry, and gave their charity. The young people were there too, and had dancing, bowling, shooting at butts, etc. ; the ancients sitting gravely by and looking on. All things were civil and without scandal."

At these Whitsun Ales there were chosen a Lord and Lady of Yule, or Ale King and Queen, who were attended by a steward, sword-bearer, purse-bearer, and mace-bearer, with their several badges or ensigns of office. They had, besides, a page or train-bearer, and a jester dressed in a parti-colored jacket; and with this mock court, they maintained such state and ceremony as their means would permit, presiding over the sports and pastimes of the festival. Sometimes holding this court of theirs in an extensive empty barn or other building suitable for the purpose, extemporized for the occasion into something like an ancient baronial hall.

"The last rural queen of this description," says the "Lancashire Folk Lore," "chosen at Downham, is still living (1867) in Burnley. The lot always fell on these occasions, it is said, to the prettiest girl in the village. A committee of young men made the selection ; then it appears an iron crown was procured and dressed with flow-

ers. The King and Queen were ornamented with flowers, a procession was then formed, headed by a fiddler. This proceeded from the inn to the front of 'Squire Asheton's,' Downham Hall, and was composed of javelin men, and all the attendants of royalty. Chairs were brought out of the hall for the King and Queen, ale was handed round, and then a dance was performed on the lawn, the King and Queen leading off. The procession next passed along through the village to the green, where seats were provided for a considerable company. Here again the dancing began, the King and Queen dancing the first set. The afternoon was spent in the usual games, dances, etc. On the next night all the young people met at the inn on invitation from the King and Queen; each paid a shilling towards the 'Queen's Posset.' A large posset was then made and handed round to the company. After this, the evening was spent in dancing and merry-making."

Rural festivals at this season, similar to the above, are still observed in Germany, where it is said:[1] —

"In the country, and among the peasantry everywhere, they dance around the *May-pole* at Whitsuntide, as in England, and maidens awake in the morning to find their windows and doors hung with wreaths of evergreen and flowers, signs of their lovers' truth. Not one but many poles may be seen in every village, dressed from top to bottom, and also little arbors in front of every door, called lovers' bowers, in which they sit and sing, or dance and play. They seek everywhere for this occasion, birchen boughs, and if the festival comes and the leaves of the birch are not yet green, there is great lamentation, and if there is only the slightest appearance of green upon the twigs, they are preferred to all other trees of the forest to hang over the windows and adorn their rooms."

[1] *Peasant Life in Germany.*

CHAPTER XIII.

MAY-DAY.

THE May-day customs referred to in the foregoing chapter are supposed by some antiquarians to have originated in the Roman Festival of Flora, which began on the 28th of April, and continued through several days in May, with various ceremonies and rejoicings, and offerings of Spring flowers, and the branches of trees in bloom. The sports and pastimes of the Whitsun Ales appear to have been for the most part merely a repetition of the

May-day games; indeed the latter appear frequently to have been transferred to the former. And the sports and pastimes of May-day were repeated at the Whitsun Ales.

Mr. Soane and others maintain that the May-day festival has come down to us from the Druids, and that this is proved by many striking facts and coincidences, and by none more so than by the vestiges of the worship of the god Bel, the Apollo or Orus of other nations. The Druids celebrated his worship on the first of May, by lighting, in honor of him, immense fires upon the various cairns.

Whether the May-day festival be either of Druidical or Roman origin, or, as Tollet imagines, derived from our Gothic ancestors, who also welcomed the First of May with songs and dances, and many rustic sports, appears to be yet undetermined. However this may be, it appears that its origin is to be sought in other countries and in far more remote periods. Maurice says, that our May-day Festival is identical with the Phallic festivals of India and Egypt, which in those countries took place upon the sun entering Taurus to celebrate Nature's renewed fertility.

At any rate, whatever may have been the heathenish origin of these May games, the May-pole long before the time of Charles I. had become so firmly rooted in the soil of Merry England, and had been, as was believed, so thoroughly divested of all its ancient idolatrous associations, as to be thought worthy even of royal and episcopal commendation; and its harmless observances were enjoined by the highest ecclesiastical authorities: —

"Our express pleasure therefore is," says King Charles I. (in the "Book of Sports"), "that after the end of Divine Service, our good people be not disturbed, letted, or discouraged from any lawful recreation, such as dancing, either men or women, archery for men, leaping, vaulting, or any other such harmless recreation; nor from having of May Games, Whitsun Ales, and Morris-dances, and the setting up of May-poles. and other sports therewith used, so as the same be had in due and convenient time, without impediment or neglect of Divine Service."

But whatever may have been the relish with which high church divines read forth to their people from the sacred desk these royal injunctions; and however much their observance may have been associated with the sentiments of religion and loyalty; still their celebration, it is well known, gave great offense to that part of their congregations who felt scruples of conscience in regard to the use of these games. For in the eyes of our Puritan forefathers, they were simply "heathen abominations." In response to the King's declaration in the "Book of Sports," we find the defiant puritanical Parliament of 1643 enacting as follows: —

"And because the profanation of the Lord's Day hath been heretofore greatly occasioned by May-poles (a heathenish vanity, generally abused to superstition and wickedness), the Lords and Commons do further order and ordain, that all and singular Maypoles, that are or shall be erected, shall be taken down and removed by the constables, borsholders, tythingmen, petty-constables, and church-wardens of the parishes where the same be; and that no May-pole shall be hereafter set up, erected or suffered to be, within this Kingdom of England, or Dominion of Wales."

Moreover, Thomas Hall, the celebrated non-conformist divine, in his "Funebria Floræ, or Downfall of May-Games," in a solemn arraignment, brings in twenty arguments in the form of theses against poor Flora, with a brief dissertation upon each, and ends by trying her before a packed jury of his own Puritans, who, as a matter of course, bring her in guilty, when the parson, as judge, thus pronounces sentence: —

"Flora, thou hast been indicted, by the name of Flora, for bringing in abundance of misrule and disorder into Church and State; thou hast been found guilty, and art condemned both by God and man, by Scriptures, fathers, councils, by learned and pious divines, both old and new, and therefore I adjudge thee to perpetual banishment."

Old Stubbs, also, as usual, is extremely eloquent on this subject: —

"Against Maie Whitsondaie, or some other tyme of the yeare, every parishe, toune or village, assemble themselves together, bothe men women and children, olde and young, even all indifferently; and either goyng alltogether, or devyding themselves into companies, they goe some to the woods and groves, &c., some to the hilles and mountaines, some to one place, some to an other, where they spende all the night in pleasant pastymes; and in the mornyng they returne, bringing with them birch boughs and braunches of trees to deck their assemblies withall. And no marvaile; for there is a great lord present amongst them as superintendent and lorde over their pastymes and sportes ; namely, Sathan, prince of Hell. But their chiefest jewell they bring from thence is their *Maie-pole*, which they bring home with great veneration, as thus : they have twentie or fourtie yoke of oxen, every oxe havying a swete nosegaie of flowers tyéd on the tippe of his hornes, and these oxen drawe home this Maie-pole — this stinking idoll rather — which is covered all over with flowers and herbes bounde rounde aboute with stringes, from the top to the bottome, and sometyme painted with variable colours (black and yellow), with twoo or three hundred men women and children followyng it with great devotion. And this beyng reared up, with handkerchiefes and flagges streamyng on the toppe, they strawe the grounde aboute, beside green boughes aboute it; set up summer haulles, bowers and arbours hard by it, and then fall they to banquet and feast, to leap and daunce about it, as the heathen people did at the dedication of their idolles, whereof this is a proper patterne, or rayther the thynge itself."

It is curious enough to contrast the effusions of this rabid fanatic, with the pleasing picture of the same custom left to us by Stowe : —

"In the moneth of May," says the cheerful old man, "namely on May-day in the morning, every man, except impediment, would walk into the sweete meadows and green woods, there to rejoyce their spirites, with the beauty and savour of sweete flowers, and with the harmony of birds praysing God in their kind ; and for example hereof Edward Hall hath noted that K. Henry the Eight, as in the 3 of his reigne and divers other years, so namely on the seventh of his reigne on May-day in the morning with Queene Katheren his wife, accompanied with many Lords and Ladies, rode a Maying from Greenwitch to the high ground of Shooter's hill, where as they passed by the way, they espied a company of tall yeomen clothed all in Greene, with greene whoodes and with bowes and arrowes to the number of 200. One being their chieftaine was called Robin Hoode, who required the king and his companie to stay and see his men shoote, whereunto the king graunting, Robin Hoode whistled, and all the 200 archers shot off, losing all at once; and when he whistled againe, they likewise shot againe; their arrowes whistled by craft of the head, so that the noyse was strange and loude, which greatly delighted the king, queene and their companie. Moreover, this Robin Hoode desired the king and queene, with their retinue, to enter the greene wood, where, in harbours made of boughes and decked with flowers, they were set and served plentifully with venison and wine by Robin Hoode and his meynie, to their great contentment, and had other pageants and pastimes."

"I find also, that in the moneth of May, the citizens of London, of all estates, lightly in every parish, or sometimes two or three parishes joyning togither, had their several Mayings, and did fetch in May-poles, with divers warlike shewes, with good archers, moricedaunters, and other devices, for pastime all the day long, and towards the evening they had stage playes and bonefires in the streetes. Of these Mayings we reade, in the raigne of Henry the Sixt, that the aldermen and shiriffes of London being, on May-day, at the Bishop of London's wood, in the parish of Stebunheath, and having there a worshipfull dinner for themselves and other commers, Lydgate the poet, that was a monk of Bury, sent to them by a pursivant a joyfull commendation of that season, containing sixteen staves in meter royall, beginning thus:—

"Mightie Flora, goddesse of fresh bowers,
Which clothed hath the soyle in lustie greene,
Made buds spring, with her sweete showers,
By influence of the sunny-shien"

So late as the end of the seventeenth century, on the morning of the 1st of May, it is said "young ladies and even grave matrons, repaired to the fields to gather May-dew with which to beautify their complexions; milkmaids also danced in the streets with their pails wreathed with garlands, and a fiddler going before them."

Says Strutt, at the beginning of the present century,—

"The Mayings are in some sort yet kept up by the milk-maids in London, who go about the streets with their garlands, music, and dancing; but this tracing is a very imperfect shadow of the original sports."

A good idea of the hilarity of the occasion may be gathered from a curious old ballad in the "Westminster Drollery," called the "Rural Dance about the Maypole:"—

"Come lasses and lads, take leave of your dads,
  And away to the May-pole hie;
For every *he* has got him a *she*,
  And the minstrel is standing by;
For Willy has gotten his Jill, and Johnny has got his Joan,
To jig it, jig it, jig it, jig it up and down.

"'Strike up,' says Wat. 'Agreed,' says Kate,
  And, 'I prithee, fiddler, play;'
'Content,' says Hodge, and so says Madge,
  'For this is a holiday!'
Then every man did put his hat off to his lass,
And every girl did curchy, curchy, curchy on the grass.

"'Begin,' says Hall. 'Aye, aye,' says Mall,
  'We'll lead up *Packington's Pound:*
'No, no,' says Noll; and so says Doll,

'We'll first have *Sellenger's Round.*'
Then every man began to foot it round about,
And every girl did jet it, jet it, jet it in and out.

" ' You're out,' says Dick. ' 'Tis a lie,' says Nick ;
 ' The fiddler played it false ; '
' 'Tis true,' says Hugh ; and so says Sue,
 And so says nimble Alse.
The fiddler then began to play the tune again,
And every girl did trip it, trip it, trip it to the men."

The morris-dance, the peculiar sport and pastime of May-day and Whitsuntide, is generally supposed to be of Moorish origin, derived from Spain. Hence its name. In confirmation of this opinion, we are told by Junius, that at one time the dancers blackened their faces to resemble Moors. Strutt, indeed, thinks differently; but his arguments, which are not very strong in themselves, seem to be altogether set aside by the fact of the word *morris* being applied in the same way by other nations to express a dance, that both English and foreign glossaries alike ascribe to the Moors. That the dance is not exactly the same as the fandango, the real Morisco, can by no means be considered as invalidating this argument, for similar deviations from originals have taken place in other borrowed amusements.

From whatever source the morris-dance may have been derived, it would seem to have been first brought into England about the time of Edward III., when John of Gaunt returned from Spain. It was certainly popular in France, as early as the fifteenth century, under the name of Morisque, which is an intermediate step between the Spanish *Morisco* and the English *morris*. There does not appear to be any mention of this dance by English writers or records before the sixteenth century; but then, and especially in the writers of the Shakespearean age, the allusions to it become very numerous. It was probably introduced into England by dancers both from Spain and France; for in the earlier allusions to it in English, it is sometimes called the Morisco and sometimes the Morisce or Morisk.

Tabourot, the oldest and most curious writer on the art of dancing, says, that in his youthful days, about the beginning of the sixteenth century, it was the custom in good society for a boy to come into the hall when supper was finished, with his face blackened, his forehead bound with white or yellow taffeta, and bells tied to his legs. He then proceeded to dance the Morisco, the whole length of the hall backward and forward, to the great amusement of the company. This was the ancient and uncorrupted morris-dance.

In England, however, it seems to have been very soon united with an older pageant-dance, performed at certain periods in honor of Robin Hood and his outlaws; and thus a morris-dance consisted of a certain number of characters limited at one time to five, but varying considerably at different periods.

There was preserved in an ancient mansion at Betley, in Staffordshire, some years ago, and it may exist there still, a painted glass window of apparently the reign of Henry VIII., representing in its different compartments the several characters of the morris-dance. George Tollett, Esq., who possessed the mansion at the beginning of this century, and who was a friend of the Shakespearean critic Malone, gave a lengthy dissertation on this window, with an engraving. Maid Marian, the Queen of May, is there dressed in a rich costume of the period referred to, with a golden crown on her head, and a red pink in her left hand, supposed to be intended as the emblem of Summer: —

"This Queen of May is supposed to represent the goddess Flora of the Roman festival; Robin Hood appears as the lover of the Maid Marian. An ecclesiastic also appears among the characters in the window, in the full clerical tonsure, with a chaplet of red and white beads in his right hand; his corded girdle and his russet habit denoting him to be of the Franciscan order, or one of the Gray Friars; his stockings are red; his red girdle is ornamented with a golden twist and with a golden tassel."

This is supposed to be Friar Tuck, a well-known character of the Robin Hood ballads. The Fool, with his cock's comb and bauble, also takes his place in the figures in the window; nor is the taborer wanting, with his tabor and pipe, "nor has the hobby-horse been forgot."[1]

[1] At Banbury there is annually exhibited a pageant, in which a fine lady on a white horse, preceded by Robin Hood and Little John, Friar Tuck, a company of archers, bands of music, flags and banners, passes through the principal street to

We may infer from the extraordinary longevity of those skilled in the morris-dances, that the exercise was conducive to the health of the body at least, if not equally so to that of the soul; the believers in "muscular Christianity," however, may reasonably doubt whether what was so good for the body, could be after all, as the Puritans maintained it was, so detrimental to the highest interests of morality.

Sir William Temple thus mentions a morris-dance which took place in Herefordshire, in King James' time : —

"There went about the country a sett of Morrice dancers, composed of ten men, who danced a Maid Marrian, and a tabor and pipe ; these ten, one with one another made up twelve hundred years. Tis not so much that so many in one country should live to that age, as that they should be in vigor and humour to travel and dance."

About a century ago, also, a famous May-game or morris-dance, was performed by eight men in the same county, whose ages computed together amounted to eight hundred years.

Brady, in his "Clavis Calendaria," published in London in 1812, says of "the May Pole, that it is still retained in most of our villages," and that, "the May-

the Cross, where the lady (Maid Marian) scatters Banbury cakes among the people. This Cross, so celebrated in the nursery hymn, "Ride a cock horse to Banbury Cross," pulled down by the Puritans in the reign of Elizabeth, has recently been rebuilt by the Banburians, to commemorate the marriage of the Princess Royal with the Crown Prince of Prussia.

games were also once so general in England, that even the priests,[1] joining with the people, used to go in procession to some adjoining wood on the May morning, and return in triumph with the much prized pole, adorned with boughs, flowers, and other tokens of the Spring season.

> " Happy the age, and harmless were the days
> (For then true love and amity was found),
> When every village did a May-pole raise,
> And Whitsun Ales and May-games did abound ;
> And all the lusty yonkers, in a rout,
> With merry lasses daunc'd the rod about ;
> Then Friendship to their banquets bid the guests,
> And poore men far'd the better for their feasts.
>
> " The lords of castles, mannors, towns, and towers,
> Rejoic'd when they beheld the farmers flourish,
> And would come downe unto the summer bowers,
> To see the country gallants daunce the morrice."

The May-pole, once fixed, remained until the end of the year, and was resorted to at all other seasons of festivity, as well as during May. Hence the general term of " May-games," to which reference is made in the " Book of Sports " and other contemporaneous writings. Some of these poles, made of wood of a more durable nature, remained for years, being merely

---

[1] Dr. Parr was a great patron of May-day festivities. Opposite his parsonage house at Watton near Warwick, stood the parish May-pole, which was annually dressed with garlands, and the doctor himself danced with his parishioners around the shaft.

freshly ornamented instead of being removed, as was the common practice. The last of such permanent May-poles in London was taken down in 1717, and conveyed to Wanstead, in Essex, where it was fixed in the park for the support of an immensely large telescope. Its original height was upward of one hundred feet above the surface of the ground, and its station on the east side of Somerset House has been thus commemorated by Pope:—

> "Amidst the area wide they took their stand,
> Where the tall May-pole once o'erlook'd the Strand."

The May-pole in later times in this country, appears to have been transformed into the Liberty-pole.

The third canto of Trumbull's "McFingal" is called the "Liberty-Pole." When the hero caught sight of it and the crowd around it, he exclaimed:—

> "What mad-brained rebel gave commission
> To raise this *May-pole* of sedition."

We may infer from the above that Trumbull thought that the May-pole, around which in England young people had joyful gatherings, suggested our Liberty-pole first raised in New York, in 1766, and which has been erected in all parts of this country as a rallying point for public meetings and Fourth of July celebrations.

Another May-day custom worthy of notice, is still

kept up at Oxford. On the top of the magnificent tower of Magdalen College, an anthem is sung at sunrise every May morning. The choristers and singing men of the College Chapel in their surplices, assemble there a little before five o'clock, and as soon as the clock has struck, commence singing their matins.

The college, it appears, holds certain land on condition of the annual performance of this ceremony, which, by the way, is said to be a substitute for a mass or requiem, which before the Reformation used to be annually sung in the same exalted position, for the rest of the soul of Henry VII. the founder of the college. The beautiful bridge, and all around the college, is covered with spectators, the inhabitants of the city as well as the neighboring villages collecting together, some on foot, and some in carriages, to hear the choir, and welcome in the happy day. The effect of the singing is said to be sweet and solemn, and almost supernatural, and during its celebration the most profound stillness reigns over the assembled numbers; all seem impressed with the angelic softness of the floating sounds, as they are gently wafted down by each breath of air. All is hushed and calm and quiet — even breathing is almost forgotten, and all seem lost even to themselves, until with the first peal of the bells (of which there are ten) the spell is broken, and noise and confusion usurp the place of silence and quiet.

CHAPTER XIV.

ST. JOHN'S, OR MIDSUMMER'S EVE.

THE history of the Church Ales, which it is one purpose of the present work to illustrate, could not, it is thought, be considered satisfactory or complete, without at least a brief account of those brilliant midsummer festivities celebrated on the Eve of St. John Baptist's Day, or Midsummer's Eve.

St. John Baptist's Day has been throughout the

greater part of Christendom one of the most popular of the Church festivals.

The observances connected with the Nativity of St. John, says the " Book of Days," " commenced on the previous evening, called as usual the Eve, or Vigil, of the festival, or Midsummer Eve; when the people were accustomed to go into the woods and break down branches of trees, which they brought to their homes, and planted over their doors, amidst great demonstrations of joy, to make good the Scripture prophecy respecting the Baptist, that 'many should rejoice at his birth.' "

This custom was universal in England till the recent change in manners. In Oxford there was a specialty in the observance, of a curious nature. Within the first court of Magdalen College, from a stone pulpit at a corner, a sermon used to be preached on St. John's Day; at the same time the court was embowered with green boughs and flowers, that the preaching might resemble that of the Baptist in the wilderness.

It appears from the records of the college, that the payment for decorating the chapel with green boughs for the feast of St. John Baptist was made for the last time in the year 1766, for the old custom of preaching an annual sermon from the stone pulpit in St. John's quadrangle was then transferred to the chapel. Whitfield, in a pamphlet published about the year 1768, says: " They have lately thought proper to adjourn into the chapel."

ST. JOHN'S, OR MIDSUMMER'S EVE.

"At night, according to ancient custom, materials for a fire were collected in a public place and kindled. To this the name of bonfire was given, a term, of which the most rational explanation seems to be that it was composed of contributions collected as boons or gifts of social and charitable feeling. Around this fire the people danced with almost frantic mirth, the men and boys occasionally jumping through it, not to show their agility, but as a compliance with ancient custom. There can be no doubt that this leaping through the fire is one of the most ancient of all superstitions, and is identical with that followed by Manasseh. We learn that till a late period this practice was followed in Ireland on St. John's Eve."

It was customary also in towns to keep a watch walking about during the Midsummer Night, although no such practice might prevail at the place from mere motives of precaution. This custom was observed at Nottingham, as late as the reign of Charles I. Every citizen either went himself or sent a substitute, and an oath for preservation of peace was duly administered to the company at their first meeting at sunset. They paraded the town in parties during the night, every person wearing a garland of flowers upon his head, additionally embellished, in some instances, with ribbons and jewels. "This custom of wearing floral crowns appears to have been very general in old times, not only on St. John's Day, but also on other festive occasions.

Polydore Virgil says, that in England they not only decorated the church with flowers, but the priests, crowned with flowers, performed the service on certain high days, more especially at St. Paul's Cathedral in London, on the feast day of the patron Saint.

Learned John Stow also states that the ritualistic dean and chapter of that cathedral on St. Paul's Day, were "appareled in copes and vestments with garlands of roses on their heads."

"A probable relic of this custom may be traced in the fact that the judges, the Lord Mayor, the aldermen, sheriffs, and common councillors, when they attend service in great state at the cathedral on the Sunday after Easter, and on Trinity Sunday, with many of the clergy, carry each of them a boquet of flowers in their hands."

In London, on St. John's Eve, or Midsummer Night, the people illuminated their houses with clusters of lamps, and performed the ceremony of setting the city watch with great show and splendor. The watchmen were clothed for the occasion in bright harness; the Lord Mayor, the city officers, and a crowd of minstrels, henchmen, giants, pageants, and morris-dancers, formed part of the procession, over which a flood of light was poured from hundreds of blazing cressets and huge torches carried upon men's shoulders.

This general illumination and rejoicing doubtless had some reference to the Baptist; the illumination and festivity being suggested by the text, "He was a burning and a shining light; and ye were willing for a season to rejoice in his light." (John v. 35.)

Pageants of all kinds were very popular at this time in different towns, and in none more so than in the ancient city of Chester, where the Whitsuntide festivities seem to have embraced those of the proximate red-letter Day of St. John the Baptist. In the 24th Henry VIII. there was issued a proclamation made by William Nowall, clerk of the pendice, setting forth that: —

"In ould tyme not only for the augmentacyon and increes of the holy and catholick faith, and to exhort the minds of common people to good devotion and wholesome doctrine, but also for the commonwealthe and prosperity of this citty (Chester), a play and declaracyon of divers stories of the Bible, beginning with the creation and fall of Lucifer, and ending with the generall judgment of the world, to be declared and played openly in pageants in the Whitsonne wceke, was devised and made by Sir Henry Francis, somtyme mooncke there; who gat of Clement then bushop of Rome, 1000 days of pardon, and of the bushop of Chester at that tyme 40 days of pardon, to every person resorting in peaceable manner to see and heare the said plays; which were, to the honor of God, by John Arnway, then Mayor of Chester, his brethren, and the whole cominalty thereof, to be brought forth declared and played at the coste and charges of the craftsmen and occupacyons of the said city," etc.

All who disturbed them were to be accursed of the Pope till he absolved them.

The setting of the "watch" on St. John's Eve at Chester, appears to have been a very showy exhibition, which at one time was greatly objected to on the alleged score of immorality; but this objection was overruled by the anti-puritanical authorities of Queen Elizabeth's time: " Four giants, one unicorn, one dromedary, one luce, one camel, one ass, one dragon, six hobby-horses, and sixteen naked boys," were included in the pageants. At this time (1564) it appears that such quantities of pasteboard cloth and other materials were required for building up the giants to a proper size, that these alone cost five pounds a head, equal to three times that amount at the present day. Another of the items is still more curious: "Two shillings' worth of arsenic" had to be mixed with the paste to save the giants from being devoured by the rats.

Strutt remarks that pageants, though commonly exhibited in the great towns and cities of England on solemn and joyous occasions, were more frequent in London than elsewhere on account of its being the theatre for the entertainment of foreign monarchs, and for the procession of the kings and queens to their coronation. At the coronation of Queen Elizabeth, on Sunday, January 15th, 1559, her progress was marked by superb pageants. On her arrival at Temple Bar, Gog and Magog, two giants, those famous worthies of Guildhall memory, were seen holding above the gate a table, wherein was written in Latin verse the effect of all the pageants which the city before had erected.

On these extraordinary occasions, the fronts of the houses in the streets through which the processions passed were covered with rich adornments of tapestry, arras, and cloth of gold; the chief magistrates and most opulent citizens usually appeared on horseback in sumptuous habits, and joined the cavalcade, while the ringing of bells, the sound of music from various quarters, and the shouts of the populace, nearly stunned the ears of the spectators.

The encouragement that literature and the Greek language received from Queen Elizabeth, created a fashion for classical allusions upon every convenient occasion, and the Queen's admiration of this kind of compliment, caused the mythology of ancient learning to be introduced into the various shows and spectacles in her honor. Wharton says, that when she paraded through a country town, almost every pageant was a pantheon. When she paid a visit at the house of any of her nobility, on entering the hall she was saluted by the Penates, and conducted to her privy-chamber by Mercury: in the afternoon, when she condescended to walk in the garden, the lake was covered with tritons and nereids; the pages of the family were converted into wood-nymphs, who passed from every bower; and the footmen gamboled over the lawn in the figure of satyrs.

To conclude this subject we give a very graphic and characteristic description, by a poet of the seventeenth century (1616), of a London marching watch on St. John's Eve. There is something grand and sublime in the idea of thus heralding in, as it were, the Nativity of the Baptist, at whose birth it was said "many shall rejoice," and who was the destined fore-

runner of Him "whose goings forth have been of old," and whose kingdom was to be "an everlasting kingdom, that all people, nations, and languages should serve him:"—

> "The wakeful shepherd by his flock in field,
> With wonder at that time far off beheld
> The wanton shine of thy triumphant fiers,
> Playing upon the tops of thy tall spiers:
> Thy goodly buildings, that till then did hide
> Their rich array, open'd their windowes wide,
> Where kings, great peeres, and many a noble dame,
> Whose bright, pearl-glittering robes did mock the flame
> Of the night's burning lights did sit to see
> How every senator, in his degree
> Adorn'd with shining gold and purple weeds,
> And stately mounted on rich trapped steeds,
> Their guard attending, through the streets did ride
> Before their foot-bands, graced with glittering pride
> Of rich-guilt armes, whose glory did present
> A sunshine to the eye, as if it meant
> Amongst the cresset lights shot up on hie,
> To chase darke night for ever from the skie,
> While in the streets the stichelers to and fro,
> To keep decorum, still did come and go;
> While tables set were plentifully spread,
> And at each doore neighbor with neighbor fed."

The bonfires, popular superstitions, and practices noticed in the beginning of this chapter, are said to be principally, if not altogether, of heathen origin. Henderson says, that—

> "From the beginning the Church appears *practically* to have tol-

erated such parts of the old mythological system as she considered harmless, and to have permitted them to live on without check or rebuke. The mass of the clergy also being of the people, were consequently imbued with the same prejudices, feelings, and superstitions as those to whom they ministered." "Perfectly unacquainted with the laws that govern the universe, the early Christians, like the Pagans and Neo-Platonists, made supernatural beings the special cause of all the phenomena of Nature. They attributed to these beings, according to their beneficial or injurious effects, all atmospheric phenomena; according to them, angels watched over the different elements, and demons endeavored to overthrow their power."

The early Fathers of the Church, in their controversy with their Pagan opponents, did not deny the existence of these "gods," but rather maintained the Scriptural doctrine that the gods which the heathen worshipped were in reality demons or devils: "They sacrificed unto devils, not to God; to gods whom they knew not." (Deut. xxxii. 17.) The conversion of our heathen ancestors to Christianity, it seems, was not so complete as to have entirely eradicated their belief in the influence and power of their ancient deities. Hence the still popular belief in omens, divinations, and enchantments of different kinds, especially those formerly practiced at the summer solstice.[1]

Durand, speaking of the rites of the Feast of St. John the Baptist, informs us of this curious circum-

---

[1] It is said that almost if not quite up to the present time, on holiday eves, the Norwegian peasant offered cakes, sweet porridge, and libations of wort or buttermilk, on mounds consecrated to the invisible folk, and called "bœttir mounds."

stance; that in some places they roll a wheel about, to signify that the sun, then occupying the highest place in the zodiac, is beginning to descend. And in the amplified account of these ceremonies given by the poet Naogeorgius, we read that this wheel was taken up to the top of a mountain and rolled down from thence; and that, as it had been previously covered with straw twisted about it and set on fire, it appeared at a distance as if the sun had been falling from the sky. And he further observes, that the people imagine that all their ill-luck rolls away from them together with this wheel.

But all such practices as these were strictly forbidden by the early Fathers, and by the general and provincial councils of the Church, on the ground that they were in reality an appeal to the false gods of their ancestors.

Moreover the influence of demons may have been thought by the superstitious to be especially great on the eve of the Nativity of the Baptist, who was declared by the Scripture to be the forerunner of Him who was to be the destroyer of the "Prince of the power of the air," and of all the "powers of darkness." (Luke xxii. 53.)

However this may be, the "marching watch" on St. John's Eve certainly was not instituted on account of any disturbed state of the country on this particular night. Indeed this warlike demonstration, and especially the white armor worn on these occasions, symbolize the spiritual armor commanded to be put on by St. Paul: "For we wrestle not against flesh and blood, but against principalities, against powers, against the rulers of the darkness of this world." This belief in the unseen world, and in the powers of darkness on this particular eve, was once very general in most European countries.

Washington Irving refers to the superstition in the "Alhambra," in the legend of Governor Manco and the Soldier. All Spain is declared by the historian, to be —

"A country under the power of enchantment. There is not a mountain cave, not a lonely watch-tower in the plains, nor ruined castle on the hills, but has some spell-bound warriors sleeping from age to age within its vaults, until the sins are expiated for which Allah permitted the dominion to pass for a time out of the hands of the faithful. Once every year, on the Eve of St. John, they are released from enchantment from sunset to sunrise, and permitted to repair here to pay homage to their sovereign Boabdil; and the crowds which you beheld swarming into the cavern are Moslem warriors, from their haunts in all parts of Spain."

In the Neapolitan towns, says the author of "Roba di Roma" —

"Great fires are built on this festival, around which the people dance, jumping through the flames, and flinging themselves about in every wild and fantastic attitude. And if you would have a medicine to cure all wounds and cuts, go out before daylight, and pluck the little flower called *pilatro* (St. John's wort), and make an infusion of it before the sun is up; but at all events, be sure on the

ST. JOHN'S, OR MIDSUMMER'S EVE.

eve of this day to place a plate of salt at the door, for it is the witches' festival, and no one of the tribe can pass the salt to injure you without first counting every grain, a task which will occupy the whole night, and thus save you from evil. Besides this, place a pitchfork, or any fork, by the door, as an additional safeguard, in case she calls in allies to help her count."

The author of the "Comical Pilgrim's Pilgrimage into Ireland," 1723, also observes:—

"On the Vigil of St. John the Baptist's Nativity, they make bonfires, and run along the streets and fields with wisps of straw blazing on long poles, to purify the air, which they think infectious, by believing all the devils, spirits, ghosts, and hobgoblins fly abroad this night to hurt mankind."

The popular superstition in regard to Christmas Eve is in pleasing contrast to the foregoing direful picture of the spiritual condition of Ireland:—

" And then, they say, no spirit can walk abroad ;
The nights are wholesome ; then no planets strike,
No fairy takes, nor witch hath power to charm ;
So hallowed and so gracious is the time." — *Shakespeare.*

The author quoted above, on the superstitions of Ireland, thus continues his account with great disgust: "Furthermore, it is their dull theology to affirm the souls of all people leave their bodies on the eve of this feast, and take their ramble to that very place, where, by land or sea, a final separation shall divorce them for evermore in this world."

This "dull theology of theirs," however, seems to

have still its zealous advocates, even in our enlightened age; for the spirit-rappings and table-turnings of these days are not only remarkable in themselves, as a proof of a return to something like a belief in the superstitions of our forefathers, but are, perhaps, but a preliminary step to a general revival of the belief in demonology, and even the practice of witchcraft; and hobgoblins and sprites may yet be conjured up from the depths of that Red Sea where the exorcisms of our pious puritanical forefathers have laid them.

Among the enchantments which were once practiced on Midsummer Eve, by young maidens in search of suitable partners for life, was that of gathering for magical purposes the rose, St. John's wort (*Hypericum pulcrum*), vervanis, trefoil, rue, and fern seed (it was thought that to possess this seed, not easily visible, was a means of rendering one's self invisible). Young women likewise sought for what they called pieces of coal, but in reality, certain hard, black, dead roots, often found under the living mugwort, designing to place these under their pillows, that they might dream of their lovers. Says Aubrey:—

"The last summer, on the day of St. John Baptist (1694), I accidentally was walking in the pasture behind Montague House; it was twelve o'clock. I saw there about two or three and twenty young women, most of them well habited, on their knees very busie, as if they had been weeding. I could not presently learn what the matter was; at last a young man told me that they were looking for a coal under the root of a plantain, to put under their heads that night, and they should dream who would be their husbands. It was to be found that day and hour."

We may suppose from the following version of a German poem, entitled the "St. John's Wort," that precisely the same notions prevail amongst the peasant youth of Germany:—

"The young maid stole through the cottage door,
And blush'd as she sought the plant of power:
'Thou silver glow-worm, O lend me thy light,
I must gather the mystic St. John's wort to-night—
The wonderful herb, whose leaf will decide
If the coming year will make me a bride.'
 And the glow-worm came
 With its silvery flame,
 And sparkled and shone
 Through the night of St. John.
And soon has the young maid her love-knot tied.
 With noiseless tread,
 To her chamber she sped,
Where the spectral moon her white beams shed;
'Bloom here, bloom here, thou plant of power,
To deck the young bride in her bridal hour!'
But it droop'd its head, that plant of power,
And died the mute death of the voiceless flower;
And a withered wreath on the ground it lay,
More meet for a burial than bridal day.
And when a year was past away,
All pale on her bier the young maid lay;
 And the glow-worm came
 With its silvery flame,
 And sparkled and shone

> Through the night of St. John,
> As they closed the cold grave o'er the maid's cold clay."

The Orpine plant, sometimes called "midsummer man," also occurs among the following love divinations on Midsummer Eve, preserved in the "Connoisseur:"—

"I and my two sisters tried the dumb cake together; you must know, two must make it, two bake it, two break it, and the third put it under each of their pillows (but you must not speak a word all the time) and then you will dream of the man you are to have. This we did, and, to be sure, I did nothing all night but dream of Mr. Blossom. The same night exactly at twelve o'clock, I sowed hemp-seed in our back yard, and said to myself: 'Hemp-seed I sow,[1] hemp-seed I hoe, and he that is my true love come after me and mow.' Will you believe me? I looked back and saw him as plain as eyes could see him. After that I took a clean shift and wetted it, and turned it wrong side out, and hung it to the fire upon the back of a chair; and very likely my sweetheart would have come and turned it right again (for I heard his step), but I was frightened, and could not help speaking, which broke the charm. I myself stuck up two midsummer men, one for myself and one for him. Now if his had died away, we should never have come together; but I assure you his bowed and turned to mine. Our maid Betty tells me, if I go backwards, without speaking a word, into the garden upon Midsummer Eve, and gather a rose, and keep it in a clean sheet of paper, without looking at it till Christmas Day,

---

[1] The same superstition is referred to in Burns' *Halloween:*—

> "Hemp-seed, I saw thee;
> An' her that is to be my lass,
> Come after me, and draw thee
> As fast this night."

it will be as fresh as in June; and if I then stick it in my bosom, he that is to be my husband will come and take it out."

A proof of the antiquity and universality of these popular superstitions is to be found in a ring, recently discovered in a ploughed field near Cawood, in Yorkshire, which appeared from the style of its inscription to be of the fifteenth century. It bore for a device, *two orpine plants* joined by a true-love-knot, with this motto above, "*Ma fiancée velt,*" that is my sweetheart wills, or is desirous. The stalks of the plants were bent toward each other, in token, no doubt, that the parties represented by them were to come together in marriage. The motto under the ring was "*Joye l'amour feu.*"

From the first, says Mr. Henderson, the Church by the decrees of councils and the voice of her chief fathers and doctors condemned such superstition (as we have noticed above), not however on the ground of their folly, but of their impiety. It is possible, therefore, that her denunciations might go toward confirming a belief in the minds of the people in the whole fabric of superstition, as a real and powerful though forbidden thing — the "Black Art," as it was called.

A long list of popular superstitions was condemned by a council held in the eighth century at Leptines in Hainault. Pope Gregory III. also issued similar anathemas. The Capitularies of Charlemagne and his successors, repeat the denunciations of them.

About the same date similar superstitions were rebuked in Scotland by the Abbot Cameanus the Wise. In the same century, St. Eligius, Bishop of Nayon, preached against similar superstitions : —

"Above all, I implore you not to observe the sacrilegious customs of the Pagans. Do not consult the gravers of talismans, nor diviners, nor sorcerers, nor enchanters, for any sickness whatsoever. Do not take notice of auguries, or of sneezings ; do not pay attention to the songs of the birds when you go abroad. Let no Christian pay regard to the particular day on which he leaves a house or enters it. Let no one perplex himself about the new moon or eclipses. Let no one do on the calends of January (Christmas holidays) those forbidden, ridiculous, ancient, and disreputable things, such as dancing, or keeping open house all night, or getting drunk. Let no one on the Feast of St. John, or any other saint, celebrate *solstices* by dances, carols, or diabolical chants."

In the provincial Council of York, in A. D. 1466, it was declared, with St. Thomas, that "all superstition was idolatry." "On the whole," continues Mr. Henderson, "it certainly appears that the early and mediæval Churches in their *collective* form, far from consciously encouraging heathenish superstition, constantly protested against it. Individual clergy in remote districts may have taken a different line, as St. Patrick is said to have done in engrafting Christianity on Paganism with so much skill, that he won over the people to the Christian religion before they understood the exact difference between the two systems of belief. At any rate — and jesting aside — the old superstition has lived on with marvelous vitality, and the Reformation, at least on the Continent, and in Scotland, has done little to check it. On the contrary, it would seem that the popular mind, when cut away from communion with the angelic world and saints departed, fastened the more readily upon a supernatural system of another order."

CHAPTER XV.

HARVEST-HOME.

AMONG the ancient festivals the revival of which in England in our times has met with especial favor and acceptance, is that of the Harvest-Home, a festival which, in its religious aspects at least, corresponds with our national Thanksgiving. Indeed the New England Thanksgiving, in all probability, has been derived from that of Old England, divested of course, of all such popular customs and ceremonies as may have seemed to our puritanical forefathers of the New England States either of heathen or Popish origin.

As among the ancient Jews the feast of the "Harvest-Home" was identical with the Feast of Pentecost, and as the Whitsun festival is but a continuation of this most ancient of festivals, we have reserved the consideration of its poetical and picturesque observances for this the concluding chapter.

The Jewish festival of Pentecost, says Mr. Blunt, in his "Key to the Prayer-Book," is supposed to have been instituted by God as a memorial of the day on which he gave the Law to Moses, and declared the Israelites "a peculiar treasure, a kingdom of priests, and an holy nation" (Exodus xix. 5, 6): an object of the day which makes its connection with Whitsunday, the day when the Holy Ghost descended to sanctify a new Israel for "a peculiar people and a royal priesthood," very significant. But the prominent character of the day was that of a solemn harvest festival. Fifty days previously, the first cut sheaf of *corn* was offered to God for a blessing on the harvest then about to begin. On the day of Pentecost, two loaves of the first new *bread* were offered (with appointed burnt offerings) in thanksgiving for the harvest then ended; and this aspect of the feast has also a striking significance. For, as Christ was the "Corn of Wheat" which (having "fallen into the ground and died" on the day of the Passover) had borne much fruit when it sprung up a new and perpetual Sacrifice to God on Easter Day, so the five thousand baptized on the day of Pentecost were the first offering to God of the "One Bread" of the Lord's Body. (1 Cor. x. 17.)

Not only has this Feast of Ingathering or Harvest-Home, been observed under Jewish dispensations, but it seems also that wherever throughout the earth, especially among Christian nations, there is such a thing as a formal harvest, there also appears an inclination to mark it with a festive celebration.

This festival of Ingathering has been observed in England at a much later period of the year than that prescribed by the Law of Moses, for the obvious reason that the grain crops were not ripe for the sickle in England until the end of Summer or the beginning of Autumn.

Among our forefathers, St. Rock's Day (August 16) was generally celebrated as the Harvest-Home. The festival is now, however, observed on different days, and much later in the season. The late ripening of the Indian corn in this country, may, perhaps, account for the still later observance with us of the Harvest-Home or Thanksgiving. It is to be regretted, however, that our practice of deferring this festival of Ingathering to the end of November, although convenient in some respects, deprives us of the enjoyment of many of those picturesque rural customs and ceremonies which distinguish the Harvest-Home of our ancestors. The month of October, with its gorgeous display of autumnal leaves, fruits, and flowers, would seem much more appropriate, and would be more in harmony with the usages of other Christian nations. Says the "Book of Days"—

"Most of the old harvest customs were connected with the in-gathering of the crops, but some of them began with the commencement of harvest work. Thus in the southern counties of England, it was customary for the laborers to elect from among themselves a leader, whom they denominated their 'lord.' To him all the rest were required to give precedence, and to leave all transactions respecting their work. He made the terms with the farmers for mowing, for reaping, and for all the rest of the harvest work; he took the lead with the scythe, with the sickle, and on the 'carrying-days;' he was to be the first to eat, and the first to drink, at all their refreshments; his mandate was to be law to all the rest, who were bound to address him as 'My Lord,' and to show him all due honor and respect. Disobedience in any of these particulars was punished by imposing fines according to a scale previously agreed on by 'the lord' and all his vassals. In some instances, if any of his men swore or told a lie in his presence, a fine was inflicted. In Buckinghamshire and other counties 'a lady' was elected as well as 'a lord,' which often added much merriment to the harvest season. For while the lady was to receive all honors due to the lord from the rest of the laborers, he (for the lady was one of the workmen) was required to pass it on to the lord. For instance, at drinking time, the vassals were to give the horn first to the lady, who passed it to the lord, and when he had drunk, *she* drank next, and then the others indiscriminately. Every departure from this rule incurred a fine. The blunders which led to fines, of course, were frequent, and produced great merriment.

"In the old simple days of England, before the natural feelings of the people had been checked and chilled by Puritanism in the first place, and what may be called gross Commercialism in the second, the Harvest-Home was such a scene as Horace's friends might have expected to see at his Sabine farm, or as Theocritus described in his 'Idyls.' Perhaps it really was the very same scene which was presented in ancient times. The grain last cut was brought home in its wagon called the hock-cart, surmounted by a figure formed of a sheaf with gay dressings — a presumable representation of the goddess Ceres — while a pipe and tabor went merrily sounding in front, and the reapers tripped around in a hand in hand ring, singing appropriate songs, or simply by shouts and cries giving vent to the excitement of the day.

"'Harvest-Home, Harvest-Home;
We have ploughed, we have sowed,
We have reaped, we have mowed,
We have brought home every load;
Hip, hip, hip, Harvest-Home!'

"So they sang or shouted. In Lincolnshire and other districts, hand-bells were carried by those riding on the last load, and the following rhymes were sung: —

"'The boughs do shake, and the bells do ring,
So merrily comes our harvest in,
Our harvest in, our harvest in,
So merrily comes our harvest in!
Hurrah!'

"Sometimes, the image on the cart, instead of being a mere dressed up bundle of grain, was a pretty girl of the reaping band, crowned with flowers, and hailed as *the maiden* Of this we have a description in a ballad of Bloomfield's: —

"'Home came the jovial hockey load,
Last of the whole year's crop,
And Grace among the green boughs rode,
Right plump upon the top.

"'This way and that the wagon reeled,
And never queen rode higher;

HARVEST-HOME. 169

Her cheeks were colored in the field,
And ours before the fire.'

"In some provinces — for instance in Buckinghamshire — it was a favorite practical joke to lay an 'ambuscade at some place where a high bank or a tree gave opportunity, and drench the hock-cart party with water. Great was the merriment when this was cleverly and effectively done, the riders laughing, while they shook themselves, as merrily as the rest.

"In the North of England, as the reapers went on during the last day, they took care to leave a good handful of the grain uncut, but laid down flat, and covered over; and when the field was done, the 'bonniest lass' was allowed to cut this final handful, which was presently dressed up with various sewings, tyings, and trimmings, like a doll, and hailed as a *corn baby*. It was brought home in triumph, with music of fiddlers and bagpipes, was set up conspicuously that night at supper, and was usually preserved in the farmer's parlor for the remainder of the year. The bonny lass who cut this handful of grain, was deemed the Har'st Queen."

In the ceremony described above, we are reminded of the Scripture story of Ruth, that Harvest Queen of other days.

The following examples, from the Rev. Edward Cutts' "Book of Church Decoration," are selected in illustration of the more modern usage in England, where the *religious* aspect of the Feast of Ingathering, seems to have been particularly revived: —

"At St. George's, Winkleigh, Devon, the church was reopened after restoration, for the Harvest Festival, and the church was handsomely decorated. For this purpose every farmer of the parish was asked to give a sheaf of corn for the decoration of the church, and what was not used for the purpose, would be distributed to the poor. The farmers were unanimous in complying with the request, and many offered more than was asked for. The day was kept as a general holiday, and several triumphal arches adorned the village. The church was decorated with corn and flowers, the thank-offerings of the parishioners. Long lines of ears of wheat swept round the arches of the aisles, with hop-flowers gracefully up the granite pillars; from the font, through the aisles to the chancel gleamed the golden grain, interspersed with flowers and mottoes.

"At All Saints', Lullingstone, Derbyshire, the parishioners went to church in procession, every one carrying a beautiful bouquet of geranium and wheat ears. On arriving at the church-yard gate, the band ceased playing; the harvest hymn, which follows, was sung: —

> "'Come, ye thankful people, come
> Raise the song of Harvest-Home!
> All is safely gathered in
> Ere the winter storms begin;
> God, our Maker, doth provide
> For our wants to be supplied;
> Come to God's own Temple, come;
> Raise the song of Harvest-Home!'

and so singing, clergy, choir, and people, entered the church in order. Everything spoke of the harvest. On either side the porch rested a good sheaf of wheat. Wheat sheaves, with bunches of grapes, were laid upon the white-vested altar. Every standard in nave and aisles bore its selected ears of corn; the flower-wreaths which crept round the stalls and lectern, were interlaced with the golden wheat ear. The font was surmounted with a canopy of flowers terminating in a tall floral cross.

At South Newton, Wilts, the parishioners went to church in procession; first, banners and a band of music, then three men in their smock-frocks, bearing sheaves of wheat, oats, and barley; then the Salisbury Plain Shepherds bearing their crooks, tied round with locks of wort and ribands; then the farmers, and then the laborers, two by two.

"At Paulton, Somerset, over the church-yard gate, was a pretty and tasteful design of flowers interspersed with corn and evergreens, flanked by two small sheaves of corn, one of wheat and the other of barley. Several flags floated in the breeze from the ancient tower, and during the day the bells rung merry peals.

"At East Brent, also, a loaf of the New Year's corn was presented and used for the Holy Communion. At St. John's, Leicester, the wreaths round the capitals and along the string courses, were of plaited wheat, oats, barley, and ivy, with red berries and red and blue flowers interspersed. In the decoration of the pulpit and font, evergreens, corn, scarlet and blue flowers, fern, twigs of barberry were used strung together with the branches of red barberries hanging down, and the effect is spoken of as being very successful. On the communion table were laid a group of two sheaves of wheat, with bunches of purple and white grapes, on a background of vine leaves, between the sheaves; and on the wall behind, encircling an I. H. S. of wheat ears, was a star of vine leaves, grapes, and flowers, having worked within it, in grains of wheat, the text, 'I am the Bread of Life.'"

In conclusion, we quote Herrick's felicitous description of the convivialities which attended the Harvest-Home thanksgiving of the olden time:[1]—

"Come, sons of summer, by whose toile
We are the Lords of wine and oile;
By whose tough labours, and rough hands,
We rip up first, then reap our lands,
Crown'd with the ears of corne, now come,
And to the pipe sing Harvest-Home.
Come forth, my Lord, and see the cart,
Drest up with all the country art.
See here a mankin, there a sheet,
As spotlesse pure as it is sweet;

[1] See Frontispiece.

The horses, mares, and frisking fillies,
Clad, all, in linnen white as lillies ;
The harvest swaines and wenches bound
For joy, to see the hock-cart crown'd ;
About the cart, heare how the rout
Of rural younglings raise the shout,
Pressing before, some coming after,
Those with a shout and these with laughter.
Some blesse the cart ; some kiss the sheaves ;
Some prank them up with oaken leaves ;
Some crosse the fill-horse ; some with great
Devotion stroak the home borne wheat :
While other rusticks, lesse attent
To prayers than to merryment
Run after with their breeches rent.
Well, on, brave boyes to your Lord's hearth
Glitt'ring with fire, where for your mirth
You shall see first the large and cheefe
Foundation of your feast, fat beefe ;
With upper stories, mutton, veale,
And bacon, which makes full the meale ;
With sev'rall dishes standing by,
As here a custard, there a pie,
And here all tempting frumentie.
And for to make the merrie cheere
If smirking wine be wanting here,
There's that which drowns all care, stout beere,
Which freely drink to your Lord's health,
Then to the plough, the commonwealth ;
Next to your flailes, your fanes, your fatts,
Then to the maids with wheaten hats ;
To the rough sickle, and the crookt sythe
Drink, frollick, boyes, till all be blythe,
Feed and grow fat, and as ye eat,

Be mindfull that the lab'ring neat,
As you, may have their full of meat;
And know, besides, you must revoke
The patient oxe unto the yoke,
All, all goe back unto the plough
And harrow, though they're hang'd up now.
And you must know, your Lord's word 's true,
Feed him you must, whose food fills you.
And that the pleasure is like rain,
Not sent you for to drowne your paine;
But for to make it spring againe."

Gloria in Excelsis.

GERMAN CAROL. Tune, 16th Century.

1. When Christ was born of Mary free, In Bethlehem that fair city, Angels sang with mirth and glee
2. The Shepherds saw the angels bright, They shone with such a heav'nly light, "O God's dear son is born tonight,"

GLORIA IN EXCELSIS.

The First Noel.

THE FIRST NOEL.

2 Now by a strange and sudden star,
  Three wise men went their way afar;
  And journey'd on with deep intent,
  To seek a king, where'er it went.—*Cho.*

3 The star, their guide 'twixt north and west,
  O'er Bethlem's walls at length took rest;
  And here its light, in one calm stay,
  Fell o'er the place where Jesus lay.—*Cho.*

4 The Eastern sages watch its rays,
  And silent stand in solemn gaze.
  One enters in; and, meek and mild,
  He finds the new-born heavenly child.—*Ch.*

5 In gentle bands the infant lay,
  In manger, 'mid the corn and hay;
  The Son of David's royal line
  Was born within the stalls for kine.— *Cho.*

6 Then entered in those wise men three
  And bowed their heads with bended knee;
  They knelt before the Babe Divine,
  Led to him by the faithful sign. — *Cho.*

7 Those wise men three with offering meet,
  Fall down and worship Jesus' feet;
  With offerings rich, the gifts of old,
  Rare myrrh, and frankincense, and gold. — *Cho.*

THE FIRST NOEL.

* For remaining verses, see Chapter III., page 25.

As Joseph was a Walking.

TRADITIONAL. (Somersetshire.)

* For remaining verses, see Chapter III., page 20.

The Holy Well.

THE HOLLY AND THE IVY.

BRINGING IN THE BOAR'S HEAD AT QUEEN'S COLLEGE, OXFORD.

"THE origin of the ceremony of bringing in the Boar's Head, with singing, to the high table in the hall of Queen's College, Oxford, on Christmas Day, is unknown; but it may reasonably be inferred that the custom has been observed since the foundation of the college in 1340. The Boar's Head, highly decorated with bay, holly, rosemary, etc., in a large pewter dish, is slowly borne into the hall by two strong servants of the college, who hold it up as high as they can, that it may be seen by the visitors ranged on either side of the hall. The gentleman who sings the ancient carol, or 'Boar's Head Song' (generally one of the members of the college, though sometimes one of the choir of Magdalen College), immediately precedes the Boar's Head, and as he commences the song with, 'The Boar's Head in hand bear I,' touches the dish with his right hand. Two young choristers from Magdalen College follow, to sing conjointly with many of the junior members of Queen's College, the chorus, 'Caput apri defero,' etc. The dish is carried, as before stated, to the high table, where sit the Provost, Bursar, Fellows, and others, and at which many visitors are congregated." — *Holiday Book.*

The following is from the quaint original of Winkin de Worde, printed in 1521: —

"Caput apri defero,
Reddens laudes Domino.
The Boar's head in hand bring I,
With garlands gay and rosemary;
I pray you all sing merrily,
Qui estis in convivio.

THE BOAR'S-HEAD CAROL.

"The Boar's head, I understand,
Is the chief service in this land;
Look wherever it be fande (found),
Servite cum cantico.

Be glad Lords, both more and less,
For this hath ordained our steward;
To cheer you all this Christmass,
The Boar's head and mustard!
Caput apri defero,
Reddens laudes Domino!"

This carol is still annually sung, with some innovations, at Queen's College, Oxford.

"In the window, of Horspath Church, near the pulpit, is represented in painted glass, a taberdar of Queen's College, Oxford, holding a spear, on which is a boar's head." — *Skelton.*

"Taberdars are officers peculiar (it is said) to Queen's College; their duties appertained to the refectorium, or dining hall. One of these students in office, in earlier centuries, was returning home through Shotover Forest, after a day spent in recreation, and for safety against wild things, he carried a spear. Jogging homeward leisurely, it pleased him to lull the distance with a page or two of the MS. Aristotle, which he had slung in the folds of his vestment. Thus occupied, and all insecure from foes, biped or quadruped, he was terrified to find that a savage boar was at that instant thrusting itself offensively in his path. The scholar suddenly halted. The boar did likewise. The scholar extended his jaws to raise an alarming cry, and the boar followed the example, pursuing his advantage. The man who could study Aristotle in those days was not likely to be blamed for stupidity. As quick as speech the taberdar thrust the volume, vellum, brass, and all, into the animal's throat, and then finished the business with the spear, whilst his opponent was digesting his classics.

"The scholar's patron commemorated the event in the windows of Horspath Church." — *Wanderings of a Pen and Pencil.*

The Boars-head Carol.

Arranged by E. F. RIMBAULT, LL. D.

1. The Boar's head in hand bear I, Be-
2. The Boar's head, as I un der- stand, Is the
3. Our stew ard hath pro vi ded this In

deck ed with bays and rose- ma- ry; And I pray you, my mas- ters
brav- est dish in all the land; when thus be- decked with
hon - or of the King of Bliss; Which on this day to be

THE BOAR'S-HEAD CAROL.

CHRISTMAS PLAYS.

THE old Christmas play of " St. George and the Dragon," says Mr. Hervey, is still amongst the most popular amusements of this season, in many parts of England. The Guisards in Scotland also perform a play which is of similar construction, and evidently borrowed from the same source. Sir Walter Scott, in his notes to " Marmion," speaks of this play, as one in which he and his companions were in the habit of taking parts when boys ; and mentions the characters of the old Scripture plays having got mixed up with it in the version familiar to him. He enumerates St. Peter, who carried the keys, St. Paul, who was armed with a sword, and Judas, who had the bag for contributions ; and says that he believes there was also a St. George. The confusion of characters, in all the different versions, is very great. In the Whitehaven edition given below, Saint or Prince George is son to the king of Egypt and the hero who carried all before him is Alexander. The characters in the play of St. George and the Dragon, given by Hervey, are — The Turkish Knight, Father Christmas, The King of Egypt, Saint George, The Dragon, and Giant Turpin.

The same play with slight variations is also to be found in Sandys' " Christmas Tide ; " but as the most amusing of these Christmas Plays is that of Alexander and the King of Egypt, mentioned above, it is here subjoined as a specimen.

APPENDIX.

ALEXANDER, OR THE KING OF EGYPT.

A MOCK PLAY, AS IT IS ACTED BY THE MUMMERS EVERY CHRISTMAS.

Act I.— Scene I.

Enter ALEXANDER.

ALEXANDER.

SILENCE, brave gentlemen. If you will give an eye,
Alexander is my name, I'll sing a tragedy.
A ramble here I took, the country for to see,
Three actors I have brought so far from Italy;
The first I do present, he is a noble king,
He's just come from the wars — good tidings he doth bring.
The next that doth come in, he is a doctor good,
Had it not been for him I'd surely lost my blood.
Old Dives is the next, a miser, you may see,
Who, by lending of his gold, is come to poverty.
So, gentlemen, you see our actors will go round;
Stand off a little while — more pastime will be found.

Act I.— Scene II.

Enter ACTORS.

Room, room, brave gallants — give us room to sport,
For in this room we wish for to resort —
Resort, and to repeat to you our merry rhyme;
For remember, good sirs, this is Christmas time.
The time to cut up goose-pies now doth appear,
So we are come to act our merry Christmas here;
At the sound of the trumpet and beat of the drum,
Make room, brave gentlemen, and let our actors come;
We are the merry actors that traverse the street,
We are the merry actors that fight for our meat;

We are the merry actors that show pleasant play,
Step in, thou King of Egypt, and clear the way.

KING OF EGYPT.

I am the King of Egypt, as plainly doth appear,
And Prince George he is my only son and heir.
Step in, therefore, my son, and act thy part with me,
And show forth thy fame before the company.

PRINCE GEORGE.

I am Prince George, a champion *brave* and *bold*,
For with my spear I've won three crowns of gold.
'Twas I that brought the dragon to the slaughter,
And I that gained th' Egyptian Monarch's daughter.
In Egypt's fields I prisoner long was kept,
But by my valor I from them escaped :
I sounded loud at the gate of a divine,
And out came a giant of no good design ;
He gave me a blow which almost struck me dead,
But I up with my sword, and cut off his head.

ALEXANDER.

Hold, slasher, hold! pray do not be so hot,
For in this spot thou knowest not who thou'st got ;
'Tis I that's to hash thee and smash thee as small as flies,
And send thee to Satan,[1] to make mince pies.
Mince pies hot, mince pies cold —
I'll send thee to Satan ere thou'rt three days old.
But hold! Prince George, before you go away,
Either you or I must die this bloody day ;
Some mortal wounds thou shalt receive of me —
So let us fight it out most manfully.

---

[1] In another version it is "to Jamaica."

Act II. — *Scene I.*

ALEXANDER *and* PRINCE GEORGE *fight — The Latter is wounded and falls.*

KING OF EGYPT.

Curst Christian! what is this thou hast done?
Thou hast ruined me by killing my best son.

ALEXANDER.

He gave me a challenge. How should I him deny?
And see how low he lies who was so high.

KING OF EGYPT.

O, Sambo, Sambo, help me now,
For I was never more in need,
For thee to stand with sword in hand,
And to fight at my command.

DOCTOR.

Yes, my liege, I will thee obey,
And by my sword I hope to win the day:
Yonder stands he who has killed my master's son,
And has his ruin thoughtlessly begun;
I'll try if he be sprung from Royal blood,
And through his body make an ocean flood.
Gentlemen, you see my sword's point is broke,
Or else I'd run it through that villain's throat.

KING OF EGYPT.

Is there never a doctor to be found
That can cure my son of his deadly wound?

DOCTOR.

Yes, there is a doctor to be found
That can cure your son of his deadly wound.

KING OF EGYPT.

What diseases can he cure?

DOCTOR.

All sorts of diseases,
Whatever you pleases —
The phthisic, the palsy, and gout —
If the devil were in, I'd blow him out.

KING OF EGYPT.

What is your fee?

DOCTOR.

Fifteen pounds is my fee,
   The money to lay down;
But as 'tis such an one as he,
   I'll cure him for ten pound.
I carry a little bottle of alicumpane;
   Here, Jack, take a little of my flip-flop,
   Pour it down thy lip-top,
Rise up and fight again.

                   [*The Doctor performs his cure as the scene closes.*

Act III. — Scene II.

PRINCE GEORGE (*arises*).

O, horrible, terrible! the like was never seen —
A man drove out of seven senses into fifteen,
And out of fifteen into fourscore —
O, horrible! O, terrible! the like was ne'er before.

ALEXANDER.

Thou silly ass, thou liv'st on grass;
   Dost thou abuse a stranger?
I live in hopes to buy new ropes
   And tie thy nose to a manger.

PRINCE GEORGE.

Sir, unto you I give my hand.

APPENDIX.

ALEXANDER.

Stand off, thou slave! Think thee not my friend!

PRINCE GEORGE.

A slave, sir! That's for me far too base a name —
That word deserves to stab thine honor's fame.

ALEXANDER.

To be stabbed, sir, is least of all my care —
Appoint your time and place, I'll meet you there.

PRINCE GEORGE.

I'll cross the water at the hour of five.

ALEXANDER.

I'll meet you there, sir, if I be alive!

PRINCE GEORGE.

But stop, sir, I'll wish you a wife, both lusty and young,
Can talk Dutch, French, and th' Italian tongue.

ALEXANDER.

I'll have none such!

PRINCE GEORGE.

Why? Don't you love your learning?

ALEXANDER.

Yes; I love my learning, as I love my life;
I love a learned scholar, but not a learned wife.
Stand off, etc. (*as before*).

KING OF EGYPT.

Sir, to express thy beauty I'm not able,
For thy face shines as the kitchen table;
Thy teeth are no whiter than the charcoal, etc.

ALEXANDER.

Stand off, thou dirty dog, or by my sword thou'lt die —
I'll make thy body full of holes, and cause thy buttons fly.

Act IV. — Scene I.

KING OF EGYPT *fights and is killed.*

Enter PRINCE GEORGE.

O, what is here? O, what is to be done?
Our King is slain — the crown is likewise gone.
Take up his body, bear it hence away,
For in this place it shall no longer stay.

CONCLUSION.

Bouncer! Buckler! Velvet's dear,
And Christmas comes but once a year,
Though when it comes it brings good cheer.
But farewell, Christmas, once a year —
Farewell — farewell — adieu friendship and unity,
I hope we have made sport and pleased the company.
But, gentlemen, you see we're but actors four,
We've done our best — and the best can do no more.[1]

---

[1] "These tragic performers wear white trowsers and waistcoats, showing their shirt-sleeves, and are much decorated with ribbons and handkerchiefs — each carrying a drawn sword in his hand, if they can be procured, otherwise a cudgel. They wear high caps of pasteboard, covered with fancy paper, adorned with beads, small pieces of looking-glass, bugles, etc. — several long strips of different colored cloth strung on them, the whole having a fanciful and smart effect. The Doctor, who is a sort of merry-andrew to the piece, is dressed in some ridiculous way, with a three-cornered hat and painted face."

"The Turk sometimes has a turban; Father Christmas is personified as a grotesque old man, wearing a large mask and wig, with a huge club in his hand. The female, when there is one, is in the costume of her great-grandmother. The hobby-horse, when introduced, has a sort of representation of a horse's hide, but the dragon and the giant, when there is one, frequently appear with the same style of dress as the knights."

INDEX.

Ales, or Wakes, when held, 126.
Alexander, or the King of Egypt, 189.
Ash-tree, man created out of, 11.
As Joseph was a Walking, carol, 20, 180.

Bacon, origin of the name, 75.
Banbury Cross, 141.
Beating the Bounds, 111.
    Boys, 116.
Boar's Head, bringing in of, 70, 71, 75, 184.
    origin of custom, 72, 184.
    favorite Norman dish, 72.
    carol describing the death of a boar, 72.
    ballad commemorating the death of a boar, 73.
    Dean Wade's account of the origin of, 74.
    modern observance of, 75.
    in New York and Troy, 76.
Boy Bishop, 51.
Brawn, receipt for making, 71.

Carnival. See Shrove-Tide, 90.
Carol, derivation of word, 15.
Carol for St. Stephen's Day, 18.
Christ Child, legend of, 46.
Christmas, derivation of word, 8.
    early observance of, 8.
    English observance of, 11.
    dressing of churches with evergreen, 11.
    ringing of London bells, 13.
    Noel, derivation of, 31.
    in the Halls of Old England, 33.
    how kept by Sir William Hollis, 40.

Christmas, how kept by Duke of Norfolk, 40.
    Twelfth Day, or Old Christmas, 80
    observed in King Alfred's time, 82.
Christmas Banquets, 69.
    Boar's Head, the first dish at, 70.
    by Henry VII., 70.
    at St. John's, Oxford, 1607, 71.
    at Queen's College, 71.
    Christmas pie, 76.
Christmas-block, or Yule-log, 10.
Christmas Carols, 14.
    origin of singing, 14.
    derivation of word Carol, 15.
    sung by Pifferari in Italy, 15.
    Yule songs, 16.
    Welcome Yule, 17.
    The Holy Well, 21, 181.
    Joyes Fyve, 24.
    Christmas Day in the Morning, 25, 179.
    The Holly and the Ivy, 27, 182.
    always popular in England, 29.
    revival of in recent times, 30.
    two classes, religious and convivial, 28, 32.
    the killing of the boar, 72.
    ballad of the killing of a boar, 73.
    Nay, Ivy, Nay, 96.
    Holly and Ivy, 97.
    music of, 174.

INDEX.

Christmas Day in the Morning, carol, 25.
Christmas Eve, celebrated by Luther, 46.
    in Germany, 46.
    in Pennsylvania, 46.
Christmas Gambols, 58.
    Snap-Dragon, 59.
    song of Snap-Dragon, 60.
    Lord of Misrule, 61.
    Roman Saturnalia, 61.
    at Sir Richard Evelyn's estate, 62
    described by Stubbs, 63.
    celebrated by the Templars, 66.
    by Sir F. Vivian in Cornwall, 67.
Christmas Mummeries, 45, 188.
    their disappearance, 45.
    the Christmas tree, 46.
    plays and moralities, 47.
    object of, 47.
    at court, 48.
    in the country, 50.
    Boy Bishop, 51.
    Father Christmas, 55.
Christmas Pie, 76.
    composition of, 76, 77.
    mince-pie, 78.
Christmas Tree, decorating of, 46.
    and Christ Child, 46.
Christian Festivals, their origin, 3, 4, 7.

Dancing at Easter a religious ceremony, 104.
    morris-dancing, 123, 139.
    its antiquity, 104, 140.

Easter or Eoster, 3.
Easter, derivation of word, 99.
    putting out fires, 100.
    use of flowers, 101.
    lifting or heaving, 101, 103.
    hand-ball, 103.
    dancing, 104.
    the Tansy-cake, 105.
    Pasche eggs, 106.
    blessing food, 108.
Easter Ales, 126.
Epiphany, definition of, 81.

Gospel-trees, 114.
Gothic Halls described, 33.
Gregory the Great, letter to Mellitus, 1.

Halls of Old England, 33.
    appearance of on Christmas Eve, 44.
    Gothic halls, 33.
    Norman halls, 34.
    furnishing of, 36.
    feasting in the, 39.
Harvest Home, 164.
    our Thanksgiving day, 164.
    Jewish Pentecost, 165.
    how kept in England, 167.
    in the parish churches of England, 169.
    Herrick's description, 171.
Heaving, an Easter sport, 101.
    antiquity of, 103.
Herrick, song of Twelfth Night, 88.
    Harvest Home, 171.
Holly and the Ivy, carol, 27, 182.
Holy Well, carol, 21, 181.

Jewish Festivals, 4.
Joyes Fyve, carol, 24.

King and Queen of the Bean, 86.
    song of, by Herrick, 88.
King and Queen at the Whitsun Ales, 130.

Lambs' Wool, how composed, and meaning of, 88.
Liberty Pole (McFingal), 144.
Lifting, an Easter sport, 101.
    antiquity of, 103.
Lord of Misrule, 61.
    his powers derived from Roman Saturnalia, 61.
    at Sir Richard Evelyn's estate, 62.
    described by Stubbs, 63.
    Saturnalia Roman, 61.
Loving cup, kissing of, 43.
Ludi, or plays and moralities, 48.
    at Court of Edward III., 48.

Magi, or wise men of the East, 82.
    adoration of, 85.
May-Day, 132.
    Roman Festival of Flora, 132.
    Druidical origin, 133.
    May-pole in England, 133.
    May-day sports forbidden by Parliament in 1643, 134.
    Thomas Hall's trial of Flora, 135.
    Stubbs on May-day follies, 135.
    Stowe draws a fairer picture, 136.

INDEX.

May-Day, ballad, " Rural Dance round the May-pole," 138.
    Queen of the May, 141.
    Banbury Cross, 141.
    at Magdalen College, 144.
May-Pole, 133, 143.
    in London, 1717, 144.
    McFingal's Liberty Pole, 144.
Midsummer's Eve, 146.
    celebrated at Magdalen College, 147.
    at Nottingham, 148.
    at St. Paul's Cathedral, 149.
    at Chester, 150.
    at Queen Elizabeth's Coronation, 151.
    London Marching Watch, 152.
    superstitious practices forbidden, 155.
    St. John's Eve in Spain, 156.
    St. John's Eve in Naples, 156.
    St. John's Eve in Ireland, 157.
    enchantments practiced, 158.
    love divinations, 160.
    Burns' Halloween, 160.
    the Orpine plant, 160.
    superstitions condemned, 161
Mince Pie, 78.
Miracle plays, 45.
    at court, 48, 49.
    in the country, 50.
    St. George and the Dragon, 50.
    Boy Bishop, 51.
    Father Christmas, 56.
Morris Dancing, 123.
    origin of, 139.
    first brought to England, 139.
    in times of James I., 142.
Mothering, word defined, 93.
Music —
    Gloria in Excelsis, 174.
    The First Noel, 176.
    Christmas Day in the Morning, 179.
    As Joseph was a walking, 180.
    The Holy Well, 181.
    The Holly and the Ivy, 182.
    The Boar's Head Carol, 186.

Noel, French term for Christmas, 31.
Norman Halls described, 34.

Pagan Festivals, 2.
Pancake Bell, 91.
Pasche eggs at Easter, 106.
    origin of Pasche egging, 108.

Pentecost, Jewish Festival, identical with Harvest Home, 165.
Perambulating the Parish, 111.
    observed by Hooker, 115.
Pifferari, carol-singing by, 15.
    description of, 16.
Plays and Moralities, 48.
    at Court of Edward III., 48.
    of Henry VIII., 49.

Queen of the May, 141.

Rhyne Toll of Chetwode Manor, 73.
Rogation Week, 110.
Rogation Ceremonies, origin of, 112.
    Roman Terminalia, 113.
    Gospel-trees, 114.
    processions in London, 114.
    beating the bounds, 111.
    beating the boys, 116.
    Herbert's Country Parson, 116.
    anecdote of Duke Robert, 116.
    ludicrous anecdote, 118.
    Wells of Tissington, 119.

St. George and the Dragon, 50, 188.
St. John Baptist's Day, 3.
St. John's Eve. See Midsummer's Eve, 146.
Shrove-Tide, 90.
    Taylor's description of, 91.
    at Westminster School, 91.
    carnival festivities, 92.
    going a-mothering, 92.
    game of foot-ball, 94.
    Billet, or Tip-cat, 94.
    the Holly Boy, 96.
    Nay, Ivy, Nay, carol, 96.
Simnel, how made, 93.
Snap-Dragon, 59.
    song of, 60.
Sword Dance in the North of England, 50.

Tacitus, opinion of Jewish festivals, 6.
Tansy cake, prize at game of ball, 105.
Thanksgiving, identical with Harvest Home, 164.
Three Kings of Cologne, 84.
Twelfth Day, or Old Christmas, 80.
    old and new style, 81.
    observed in King Alfred's time, 82.

Twelfth Day, or Old Christmas,
    Magi, or wise men of the East, 82.
    Three Kings of Cologne, 84.
    Rex Convivii, or Arbiter Bibendi, 85.
    Bean King and Queen, 86.
    song of, by Herrick, 88.

Waits, instruments used by, 30.
    their number in 1554, 114.
Wassail, definition of, 42.
    origin of drinking, 42.
    wassail-bowl described, 41.
    loving cup, 43.
Welcome Yule, song of, 17.
Whitsun ales, 123.

Whitsuntide, definition, 122.
    Whitsun ales, 123.
    morris dances, 123, 124.
    descent of the Holy Ghost, 125.
    wakes, or ales, when held, 126.
    selling ale in churches, 129.
    Stubbs denounces "ales," 129.
    Aubrey approves them, 130.
    games and festivals of the season, 130.
    observed in Germany, 131.
Wise men of the East, 32.
Yule, or Juul, 3.
Yule Log, bringing in of, 10, 41.
    burnt till Twelfth Night, 87.
    superstitions concerning, 88.

Zoroaster, 82.

www.ingramcontent.com/pod-product-compliance
Lightning Source LLC
Chambersburg PA
CBHW020817230426
43666CB00007B/1043